Fighting for My Life:
GROWING UP WITH CANCER

Fighting for My Life

GROWING UP WITH CANCER

Amy M. Mareck

Fairview Press
Minneapolis

Published by Fairview Press, 2450 Riverside Avenue, Minneapolis, MN 55454. Fairview Press is a division of Fairview Health Services, a community-focused health system, affiliated with the University of Minnesota, providing a complete range of services, from the prevention of illness and injury to care for the most complex medical conditions. For a free current catalog of Fairview Press titles, call toll-free 1-800-544-8207, or visit our Web site at www.fairviewpress.org.

Library of Congress Cataloging-in-Publication Data
Mareck, Amy M., 1985-2004.
  Fighting for my life : growing up with cancer / Amy M. Mareck.
    p. cm.
  ISBN 978-1-57749-168-2 (pbk. : alk. paper)
  1. Mareck, Amy M., 1985-2004—Health. 2. Cancer in children—
Patients—Biography. I. Title.
  RC281.C4M35 2007
  618.92'994—dc22
                                        2007003935

Printed in the United States of America
First printing: April 2007
12 11 10 09 08   7 6 5 4 3 2 1

Cover design by Laurie Ingram
Cover photos courtesy of Richard and Judith Mareck
Book design by Dorie McClelland, Spring Book Design

*This book is dedicated to all the children and their families
who are fighting their own battles against cancer.
May your journey be filled with no regrets,
and remember to never give up.
Fight for your life!*

Foreword

Osteosarcoma, like all cancers in children and adolescents, is a rare disease. In any given year, there are only about four hundred new cases of osteosarcoma in persons under age twenty in the entire United States. We don't know what causes this disease, why it spreads in some patients and not others, or why the same therapy may cure one patient but not another. We do know that most children with osteosarcoma will be cured of their disease, and we know that with continued research, testing, and persistence we will cure even more children in the years ahead.

Amy's story is amazing. It is a story of strength and friendship, and it exemplifies a perseverance and dignity we would all do well to aspire to. There were very few visits in the last years of Amy's life where I had the chance to deliver good news. Most of the time, it was at best "not worse" news. Yet, Amy stayed positive about every visit. Her desire to fight cancer fueled my drive to fight for her. Despite all the bad news, clinic visits, and difficult phone calls, it was always a pleasure to see Amy, and I am truly fortunate to have had any time with her at all. She was able to brighten my days and those of everyone involved in her care. She made good friends in the hospital, in the community, and even among professional athletes (who got in line with the rest of us at her memorial service).

Amy's life was ultimately cut short by a disease she certainly did not bring on herself or in any way deserve. Unfortunately, Amy's story is not unique. More children will be diagnosed with cancer tomorrow; and, like Amy, they and their families will begin a journey they could not have imagined before the diagnosis. So many of these children will be asked to mature too quickly, as they are forced into a complex world of doctors, nurses, medicines, and hospitals they can barely comprehend. Again and again, these children will show a level of courage many of us may never be asked to show. And again and again, they will inspire us to fight with them for their lives—and for the lives of all children touched by serious illness.

Joseph P. Neglia, M.D., M.P.H.
University of Minnesota Medical Center, Fairview
Minneapolis, Minnesota

Acknowledgments

This book wouldn't be a book if I didn't say thank you to a lot of people—people I came to know because of cancer, and some whom I haven't even met.

To all my nurses: There's something about each and every one of you that has left an imprint on my mind. You took care of me, comforted me, gave me a shoulder to cry on, and were there for me, always. We shared laughter, tears, and frustration, and basically rode the same roller coaster together. You were there every step of the way, fighting with me, and I knew I could always turn to you **whenever** I needed to. You were more than nurses to me; you were my friends, and I love you all. Thank you to my nurse Jill, or "Auntie Jill," who brought her little dog Coca to visit me, and to Carol, who always had lots of laughs with me in the cafeteria. To Crista, who was the best whenever I needed to cry or talk to someone. To Casey, another awesome nurse, and to Meagan, Holly, Amy, Erica, Carolyn, Josie, Stacie, Lori, and Nancy—my list could go on forever—just remember, each and every one of you was special to me. To Elisa, Mary, and Candi: Elisa, you started out being my primary nurse, and you were the best. Mary and Candi, what can I say? You're both awesome people who do an amazing job. There was also Chris, the child family life specialist, who was with me in the beginning and her replacement, Laura, a good listener who always cheered me up.

To Jody, a terrific pediatric oncology nurse practitioner: You were always there during the hard times, and you told me that it was going to be hard. You told me it was going to be long, and you never left me during it all. You made me a better person. I knew that I could always tell you anything, and you wouldn't judge me for it or look at me differently. When it came to being strong, I looked to you, my rock, and you always helped me.

And to Bob on 5B: You made every day a good one, not only because you kept my room clean but because you cared about me and always had a smile for me. Thank you!

To my doctor, "Uncle Joe": It all started when I was just thirteen years old. I knew you were going to help save my life, that we were a perfect match at fighting this. I would never give up, and you kept finding treatments. You gave me five more years after being diagnosed, and I wouldn't have had that without your help. When the times got rough, I knew I could turn to you for encouragement and hope. I knew I could trust you with my life. You're the best doctor anyone could ever have.

To the really cool med students and residents I got to know: You treated me like a person, rather than a number or a case. Many of you came to my room just to visit me or even to watch a little television late at night. Alice and Andy, you were always the first in line to play Cribbage with me. Thank you to Dr. Jeff, who I knew when he was a med student and for his first, second, and third years as a resident. Thanks to Adam, who always knew what to watch on Comedy Central, and to Dr. Murphy, Dr. Angie, and Dr. Mike.

To all the other doctors, surgeons, and residents along the way: I could name you all, but this list of acknowledgments would go on forever. You each had a hand in my fight with cancer. My case may have not been easy, but you took it on anyway, and I thank you for not giving up on me. All the surgeons literally held my life in their hands; I was at your mercy as you did your miracle work, and each time I came out for the better. You have been on my side and gave me hope—you will never know how much that meant to me.

To the rest of the staff at the University of Minnesota Medical Center, Fairview: I met so many that touched my life in some way. Each one of you is special. You made me feel comfortable being at the hospital, and you made things seem not so bad. You did what you had to do and always greeted me with a smile.

To the many friends and families I met at the hospital: You are all one of a kind and very special. I don't know what I would have done if you weren't a part of my life. You pulled me up when I was down, sat by my side during the rough times, and were there during the happy times. I have shared so many unforgettable moments with all of you.

To all my friends who have passed away: You are all in my heart and will never be forgotten. You will always be with me.

To my closest friends: I found out who my true friends were while I was fighting cancer. You were great and saw me through ups and downs, lefts and rights, and whichever way it went. You were my friends when I needed you the most. You'll be my friends forever.

To my mom and dad—Richard and Judy Mareck—and to my sister, Denise, and my brother, Andy, and to all of our extended family: You guys are the best. You always had little jokes to tell me in tense and sad times. You knew how to change the moment from bad to good. You were there every step of the way, rallying behind me each time and keeping me going. There's something about each of you that makes you the best, and you'll always remain the best.

To Jodi Graubard: You were the best editor and friend. You

came into my life like a special gift, and we hit it off from day one. You helped me get this book on the road, and it wouldn't have been written if it weren't for you. By encouraging me to write this book, you made one of my dreams come true.

To Susie Lott, Director of Care Partners, Fairview: Thank you for believing in my book and finding a publisher for it.

To all my supporters at my CaringBridge Web site: We never met in person, but know that you were a part of my life. You left messages that lifted my spirits and cheered me on. You made me feel special, you said prayers for me, and you did everything anyone could hope for. Thank you for being my support system.

Last but not least, to my readers: This journey taught me so much—above all, that the little things in life make it worth living and fighting for, whether you have cancer or not.

"Whenever I walk down the hospital halls,
I am reminded that each room has its own story,
its own unique miracles,
and a fight like no one else's."

—Amy Mareck

ALBANY, MINNESOTA, 1999

It was summer, my favorite time of year. After the long, cold winter of below-zero temperatures, I was finally able to come out of hibernation. School was out and I was on the loose, doing what I always did—playing basketball, baseball, and kick the can with the other kids in the neighborhood. I figured it was going to be a great season with family, friends, and fun.

In August, my parents and I took a much anticipated trip to Washington, D.C. This was my first time going to the East coast, and I couldn't wait to tour the White House and maybe even catch a glimpse of the president.

On the trip, we walked every day. Still, I was surprised that my right leg started to hurt for no reason. I first noticed it when walking to the Hard Rock Cafe to pick up a few gifts. The pain in my leg was intense, as if a nail were going through it. I noticed that I walked more slowly than usual and grew tired as the days went by. I told myself the pain in my leg must have been from all the walking. I thought about how I had played football the week before and wondered if I might have pulled a muscle.

My leg still hurt after we returned home. A few days later, my parents decided that I needed to see a doctor. During the appointment, I told the doctor that I might have pulled a hamstring because I had been active in so many sports during the months before our vacation in D.C. So that's what the doctor diagnosed—a pulled hamstring. He recommended that I start physical therapy. I took his advice and went to therapy for about a week and a half. The therapist massaged my leg to loosen up the muscles, but this didn't help. I thought I would have to put up with the pain until it eventually went away.

By early September, I had started practicing for the annual Punt, Pass, and Kick Competition, an event in which kids and teens compete to see who can get the football the farthest distance. Normally, I could punt a football forty to fifty yards, but this year I couldn't get it past the fifteen-yard mark. Then my right leg swelled like a balloon and hurt all the time. My dad took me back to the doctor to get an X-ray of my leg. As I lay there, so many thoughts went through my mind; I didn't know what was happening to me or why. The doctor said he would call later with the results.

I was now in eighth grade, and everything about school seemed the same as it had always been. I spent time with my friends, had fun, and did my dreaded homework. Back then, I had no idea how fast life could change.

THE FIRST OF OCTOBER was a cold and rainy Friday; it looked as though a storm could start at any moment. In the middle of an archery lesson during gym, I was called to the school office. My dad was there waiting for me.

He said he needed to take me back to the doctor's office to review the X-ray. I suddenly began to wonder if something was really wrong with me. Why would my dad leave work to take me to the doctor's office?

When we arrived at the clinic, we were escorted to a plain white room. A doctor came in holding the X-ray. When he put it up on the screen so we could view it, I felt the room turn gray. We looked at the X-ray in silence before the doctor pointed out the unusual cloudy white images around my femur. He thought that perhaps some calcium had built up around the bone, and he wanted me to go to the St. Cloud Hospital to get an MRI (magnetic resonance imaging) scan. My dad and I immediately left for St. Cloud.

Except for the sound of the radio, the car ride was extremely quiet. All the way there I thought, *What is this? What's happening?* One minute I was a normal thirteen-year-old aiming an arrow at an archery target and the next I was getting an MRI.

At the hospital, I was sent to an MRI room right away. I was put into a tubelike contraption that took pictures of my insides. The machine sounded like a jackhammer pounding on cement. The scan took about thirty minutes, and it was as if my life changed with every second.

By the end of the day, we had made an appointment with the University of Minnesota Children's Hospital, Fairview, for the following Monday to meet with both an orthopedic surgeon and an oncologist, a doctor who specializes in treating cancer.

THAT WEEKEND was the longest of my life. It was so hard waiting for answers, thinking about what could be wrong, and not knowing what was happening to me. To help pass the time, my parents and I stuck to our normal routine, which included grocery shopping and a visit to the mall. (I've always said, "When the going gets tough, the tough go shopping.") We didn't talk about what was going on. But I could tell that we all felt like we were having the same bad dream, and we wished we could wake up and have it be over.

On Monday morning, my dad and I set out for the Twin Cities of Minneapolis and St. Paul. My dad thought it would be best if my mom stayed home. He knew that if we were going to hear bad news, he would take it better than my mom could. I think he felt that it would be better for her to hear bad news from him than from a stranger.

The appointment was scheduled for the afternoon, and the drive would take two hours. We were going to the oncology clinic of the University of Minnesota Children's Hospital. As we drove, we kept the radio on for a diversion. The sun shone brightly the whole way there, which seemed odd to me because of all that was happening. I knew I had to prepare myself—I knew I needed to be strong. But nothing could have prepared me for what I was about to hear.

Never be afraid to ask for help.

Have the courage to tell your parents or someone close to you that you think something is wrong. Never ignore pain. I was afraid to go to the doctor, but I had to find out what was wrong with me. Why did my leg hurt? Why didn't I have any energy? Don't wait. The sooner you know what's happening, the sooner the doctors can help you.

UNIVERSITY OF MINNESOTA CHILDREN'S HOSPITAL, FAIRVIEW

We arrived at the hospital with my scans in hand. I was seen by Dr. Cheng, an orthopedic surgeon, and by Dr. Neglia, a pediatric oncologist. Both doctors took one look at the scan and said that a biopsy of the mass on my femur was needed as soon as possible. They explained that a biopsy is a surgical procedure that would allow them to take a small sample of the mass so they could determine exactly what it was. Both Dr. Neglia and Dr. Cheng then said it was more than likely osteogenic sarcoma, or osteosarcoma, a rare type of bone cancer.

Their words cut through me like a knife. My heart pumped madly in my chest. How, why, when could I have gotten *cancer?* The word brought chills to my spine.

The doctors reassured me that the cancer wasn't my fault—it was nothing *I* had done. Tears filled my eyes as I sat there and thought about what was happening to me. It was as if my life were falling apart right before my eyes. I sat back and took a deep breath. My dad did the same. The two of us sat there in shock.

Minutes later, I was sent to have my blood drawn so the doctors could check my "counts." They checked my platelets, cells that prevent the body from bleeding; my hemoglobin, which carries oxygen to the tissue; white blood cells, the ones that fight infection; neutrophils, other infection-fighters; and absolute neutrophil, which determines whether a patient will be able to receive a cancer treatment called chemotherapy. I'd never had blood taken before and was a little scared because I didn't like the idea of being stuck with a needle. But I put on a brave face and did it. The biopsy was scheduled for the next day.

MY DAD AND I had to be on floor 3C, the surgery waiting area, by five thirty in the morning. I was then taken back to the pre-op room where I put on a gown and continued preparations for the OR (operating room). The pre-op room had paintings on the wall and flying paper birds hanging from the ceiling. I thought they were there to help patients feel more at home. The room didn't smell like home, though. All I could smell was that weird sterile odor that only hospitals have.

I was nervous and started to get nauseated. The nurses gave me some medicine to help me relax, and two hours later it was time to go into the OR. My dad and his sister Maureen, who was there to support us, watched me go. In the OR, a mask was put on my face and within seconds, I was asleep. The procedure went fine, and then I was in recovery for a few hours after that.

OCTOBER 5, 1999, was a day I'll never forget. Dr. Neglia was very straightforward and said he was sorry but his initial diagnosis had been correct. The mass on my femur was, in fact, osteosarcoma.

Anyone who has ever sat in a doctor's office and heard the sentence, "You have cancer," knows that those words cut through your entire being. I started crying as soon as the words came out; I thought I was going to die. The air in the room seemed heavy and thick.

Dr. Neglia said that he would do everything he could to help me survive. He also told me that he would be my primary doctor and follow my case. Later that week, I would need to be admitted to 5B, the pediatric oncology floor at the University of Minnesota Children's Hospital, to begin intense chemotherapy. Dr. Neglia explained that he hoped the chemo would shrink the tumor in my leg enough for the tumor to be surgically removed. If the tumor were to shrink, this could save my leg from having to be amputated. The first few rounds of chemo would help us know what to expect.

I looked at my dad, who was trying his best to hide his pain. I could see the terror in his eyes.

Aunt Maureen, Uncle Denny, and my cousin Michelle were at the hospital that day, and they gave me a stuffed koala bear to cheer me up. They were all there to see us off as my dad and I left the hospital for Albany. Still drowsy from the anesthesia, I slept all the way back.

Be prepared to fight.

I am here to tell you that cancer is not a death sentence—it is a God-given challenge. It's *your* challenge to take control of your life and to fight for it—to put on your combat boots and march bravely in the face of fear. Have courage and a positive attitude. There is no other choice, no other way, to win this battle.

ALBANY, MINNESOTA

My older sister Denise and my mom were at home waiting for us. When my dad told them I had cancer, they both started to cry. Everyone tried to hold it together, even though we were all scared. My mom and Denise made a bowl of soup for me, but I couldn't eat. I went straight to bed with my leg wrapped up and elevated. It was a long night of restless sleep.

During the following days, I wanted to tell some of my friends about my diagnosis but I didn't know how. I decided to open up to two of my best friends, Catherine and Savannah. But when I tried to tell them, I was in tears and couldn't get the words out. I felt that if I said *cancer* out loud, then that would make it real.

I finally took a deep breath and told Catherine and Savannah that I had cancer. It was the hardest thing I'd ever had to say in my life.

There was a long silence. At first neither of them knew what to say.

After a few moments, they both told me they knew I could beat this. They said I could stay strong and kick this cancer in the butt. My tears would not stop. It felt like my world had turned upside down.

Word traveled fast around school. The following Friday, the whole school participated in an "Amy Day," where students and staff wore my favorite color, blue, to show their support. People had on blue ribbons, blue shirts, blue nail polish, blue everything. Pictures of me hung all over the junior high. I felt loved and supported, knowing that so many people cared.

5B, PEDIATRIC ONCOLOGY FLOOR, UNIVERSITY OF MINNESOTA CHILDREN'S HOSPITAL

On Thursday October 8, the fight of my life began—the fight that would drag me down, rip my insides apart, and at times crush my emotional strength. But I had to find a way to face the battle with pride and determination.

5B was bright and colorful, with an under-the-sea theme. At night, special blue lights shone through star-shaped cutouts; the blue glow helped me to feel calm and safe. The view outside my window was of the mighty Mississippi River. Still, my hospital room was nothing like my room at home, where the window had a view of our backyard birch trees and flower gardens.

My first night on the floor, I met Jody, the pediatric oncology nurse practitioner. She came to my room to talk about chemotherapy. She told me that, from now on, things wouldn't be easy. She said the chemotherapy was going to make me feel very sick sometimes, and there was the possibility of many side effects.

Then she threw me a real curveball—she said I would lose my hair. I thought, *Is she kidding?* What did she mean I would "lose my hair"? Would just some of it fall out? Would *all* of it?

Would it ever grow back? My brown hair was halfway down my back and incredibly thick, just the way I liked it. Lose my *hair?*

Jody explained that when the chemo went into the body, it not only killed bad cells but also good ones, including hair cells. I quickly realized that losing my hair was nothing compared to losing my life. Besides, it wasn't as if I really had a choice—and so I became willing to lose my hair.

Jody went on to tell me that, if things went well, it would take nine months to finish my protocol but that I should expect it to be closer to a year with delays from infections.

Nine months. Maybe a year.

THE FIRST CHEMO I had was called Adriamycin, an orange-colored liquid that looked like Kool-Aid. The nurse hooked it up to my "port," which had recently been placed under my skin in my upper chest area to receive the medications. A port has a line hanging out from it, and nurses put a needle into the line to administer the chemo and other medications for fighting nausea.

I watched as the liquid went through the line and into my body for the first time. The chemo would run continuously for five days. As I sat there, I got a weird feeling, like my mind was preparing my body for what was entering me.

My parents, my sister Denise, and my older brother Andy surrounded me when my chemo began that first night. I was glad they were there—they felt as much a part of this fight as I was.

I didn't cry that night. I knew the first chemo session would set the stage for how the others would go. I knew I had to be strong, and that's exactly what I was. I wanted to be strong for my parents as well as for myself. Although I knew they could handle it, I wanted to shield them and to keep my real feelings to myself.

The first night of treatment was difficult; I was nauseated, sick, and vomiting. After the others left, my dad stayed with me all night. He was ready to push the call button to alert the nurses whenever I showed signs of throwing up. I knew that my dad would have done anything to have made all of this go away—but he couldn't. I loved him even more for trying.

After several hours, the antinausea medication started to kick in and I felt a little better. My dad and I talked about how I was feeling physically, how many treatments I might need, and how long this ordeal might last. We talked about our concerns and how I might have gotten the cancer. My dad, who examines environmental issues for his company, feared that I'd developed cancer from the toxins in cleaning supplies and chemicals found in our own home.

I didn't think my cancer was caused by chemicals or that it was anyone's fault. I thought it happened because it was *supposed* to happen. God must have known I could handle it. I believe that if God brings you to it, He will bring you through it. You just have to play the hand of cards you are dealt.

AFTER THAT FIRST NIGHT, my family worked out a schedule so I would never be alone at the hospital. Someone would stay with me each night.

My mom was the next one on duty, and she granted my every wish. She took great care of me and did whatever she could to make me feel more at ease. Between the episodes of nausea, we played cards or watched movies. She was concerned that I wasn't eating and that when I did eat, the food usually came right back up.

My mom ran a daycare, so she was already used to running after kids—and running around after me was no different. She followed me around with a puke bucket because we never knew when I might need to throw up. The bucket was an accessory I brought everywhere during chemo, kind of like a purse.

I could tell my mom was hurting just by looking at her—but she would put on a happy face all the time. I told her that I was okay, that I was doing just fine, but my mom always sensed what I was really feeling.

One night, we actually found something to laugh about. My mom had settled into the chair that converts into a bed and, like me, she was sound asleep. All of a sudden, her bed collapsed—the top end went up, the bottom end went up, and my mom was stuck in the middle! Once I knew she was okay, I couldn't stop laughing about it.

As the days wore on, everyone tried to keep me as comfortable as possible. I never felt very good, and I never left my room. I ended up sleeping through most of the five days.

WHEN I FINALLY felt well enough to "walk the floor," I saw little bald kids running around connected to IV poles. Was this how I was going to look? It scared me a little, but I didn't let it bother me too much.

Finally, after completing my chemo treatment, I was told that I could go home. But before leaving, my dad and I had to go to the patient learning center so I could be taught how to give myself shots. Because chemotherapy would cause my blood counts to drop, putting me at risk for infection and other complications, I would need to be injected with G-CSF (granulocyte-colony stimulating factor) every day to try to keep my white blood counts up.

The instructor at the learning center asked if I planned to give myself the shots or have one of my parents do it. My dad looked at me, and I looked at him. I had never given myself a shot before, but I said, "I'll do it." I knew that I could give myself the shots more easily than my mom or dad could, because they would be more afraid of hurting me than I was.

The thirty-minute class was packed with lots of important information. I learned how to be sterile before giving myself a shot, how to draw the medication from a bottle using a needle, and how to dispose of the needle into a Biohazard Sharps container. But before I could leave the learning center, the instructor said I had to practice giving a shot on an orange. I tried it and did a good job—but that was just practice. I had no idea that next she was going to have me give *myself* a shot. She said I would need to practice injecting myself with a saline, or saltwater, solution.

I was scared, and at first my mind played tricks on me. All I could see was a huge, long needle staring back at me, even though in reality the needle was pretty small. I took a deep breath, drew back the needle, and poked the saltwater solution into my thigh. It didn't actually hurt much. In a quick ten seconds, I was done. I disposed of the needle as I had been taught. The instructor said, "Congratulations, you have passed."

With that, my dad and I were out the door.

Be willing to feel fear, be willing to trust.

People have often said to me that they didn't think they could deal with what I've been through. My response is always, "You could if you had to." *You* can if you have to. Have faith in the people around you—tell them how you feel and when you need help. Be willing to accept help, even if that's hard to do. Take comfort in others. Because of the cancer, I had to be willing to make adjustments in my life, even when I didn't want to. I had to be willing. You can, too.

ALBANY, MINNESOTA

I was so glad to be finished and happy to be going home. I had done it! I had made it through my first round of chemo.

I took advantage of the quiet car ride. The hospital had been noisy, with the IV pumps beeping and doctors and nurses coming in and out of my room all the time. On the way home that night, I slept cuddled up in a blanket in the front seat. Car rides at night always made me want to sleep and, of course, I was exhausted from the chemo.

When we arrived and I walked in the door, my mom was waiting to greet me with a big hug. I went straight to bed and slept the night away. It was great to be home in my own bed again.

IT DIDN'T TAKE LONG for the side effects of chemo to appear. By the next day, I had already developed sores inside of my mouth and throat. The sores felt kind of like canker sores; they were painful and kept me from eating.

I had to do special mouth care to try to keep my mouth clear of the sores. This was a chore I didn't like doing. The yellow, syrupy medication tasted like pure sugar, and I had to swallow it. It wasn't pleasant, but I took it anyway.

One day, when I was taking a shower, another side effect

showed up. As I stood under the running water, one of my worst fears came true: my hair started falling out. I couldn't understand why all of this was happening to me. I thought, *What did I do to deserve this?* It seemed that just when I'd learned to cope with one side effect, another would pop up.

When I got out of the shower, my mom held me and we cried together. She reassured me that the hair loss was temporary, but I was still down. That night, I slept with the blankets over my head to keep it warm.

The next few days were rough. I wore a hat all the time and kept glancing at myself in the mirror. I didn't like how I looked without hair.

Losing my hair was one of the first lessons I learned about not taking anything for granted in life. Before this happened to me, I took my hair for granted. I used to love doing my hair, but there were days when I didn't feel like dealing with it. After it started to fall out, I wished I had it back to deal with.

Nausea was another problem for me. I slept most of the time because of it. When I was awake, I took medications to try to keep the nausea under control. Still, there were many times when I threw up, which helped me feel a little better afterward. I barely ate, but I could still throw up. I couldn't believe that after all the vomiting there was still more to come up. I told myself, *Well, at least you know your stomach is working, right?*

Along with the chemo treatments, I had to have my counts taken twice a week. The doctors looked at my counts to determine whether I needed to be transfused with either blood or platelets. The doctors watched my counts closely to make sure they didn't fall too far and to learn when I would be ready for my next round of chemo. So, even when I wasn't at the hospital, the doctors kept a close eye on me.

UNIVERSITY OF MINNESOTA
CHILDREN'S HOSPITAL, FAIRVIEW

On October 28, one day before my fourteenth birthday, I was back at the hospital for a checkup with Dr. Neglia. My dad was with me. I needed to have a CT scan of my chest because if osteosarcoma spreads, it usually goes to the lungs first.

My checkup was going to be followed by a second round of chemo. I was more hesitant about starting the second round because I now knew how it would affect me. It meant another long hospital stay, getting sick, and sleeping a lot. To make matters worse, I'd be in the hospital on my birthday. I'd always had a birthday party at home with my friends—now I would turn fourteen hooked up to lines and tubes, most likely puking my guts out.

LATER THAT DAY, Dr. Cheng, the orthopedic surgeon, came into my room. I wondered why he was there. Dr. Cheng came right out and said that he had looked at the CT scan of my chest and seen lots of nodules—small tumors—in my lungs.

My dad took the doctor out of the room faster than you could blow out my birthday candles. My dad didn't want me to hear this right before my birthday—but it was too late for that. I sat there in tears as my dad and Dr. Cheng talked in the hall.

It's devastating to find out that you have cancer, but it's even worse to find out that the tumors are now in more than one part of your body.

When my dad returned, he tried to sugarcoat the situation for me, but I already knew the truth and I told him that. We didn't talk about it anymore. I sat back and focused on the TV. I decided that I wasn't going to let the news about the tumors bother me. I believed that the chemo would do its job on both the tumor in my leg and the ones in my lungs. I let go, leaving it up to the chemo and God to work their magic.

It was as if I had suddenly developed a hard outer shell that could protect me from bad news. I made up my mind that I would be able to accept whatever was thrown at me from that point on. I decided it didn't matter what I had to do—I was going to be strong, and I was going to beat this cancer.

THE SECOND CHEMO started much like the first. I had my eight-hour fluid flush, which cleared my insides and allowed the chemo to work better. I was also given medication to help prevent nausea.

I started to get sick right away during chemo, though. My nurse did everything she could to make me feel better, giving me more medication and staying by my side. She talked to me, trying to keep my mind off of my stomach, but all I really wanted to do was sleep.

Finally, after a half hour of throwing up, I did fall asleep, and that was just what I needed. The night passed. I woke to a new day—my birthday. I decided I wasn't going to spend it being sick.

THAT DAY MY AUNT, uncle, and cousin came and we carved a Halloween pumpkin. That evening, my mom, dad, Denise, and Andy were at the hospital to celebrate my birthday with me. They brought a cake and presents, and we had a good time.

It was a different birthday from any I had ever had, but I was just glad my family was with me. They did a great job of helping me enjoy my birthday, even though we were in the hospital. Later that night, we all said our good-byes and everyone left but Denise, who would keep me company through the night. I fell asleep right away, but the nurses kept waking me up to check me. I looked forward to the time when I could go home and sleep in my own bed, without being disturbed.

I HAD SOMETHING ELSE to look forward to as well—a trip to Walt Disney World over Thanksgiving, which we had planned months before. I thought of Disney World as my "happy place," and I told myself that I was going no matter what. The doctors scheduled my chemo so that I could still go on the trip, but we had to agree to return home on Thanksgiving Day. I would need to start my next round of chemo the day after that.

I might have looked sick, but inside I was fighting to live life to the fullest. Nothing on earth could cheer me up like Disney World. Miracles do happen to those who believe.

Make a "happy place" in your mind.

It's okay to make the hospital a fun place or to help make yourself happy in any way you can while you're there. Just remember, things will get better. When I was sick in the hospital, the one thing that could make me feel better was to think about Walt Disney World. Whenever I felt down during treatment, I went to my "happy place" in my head.

WALT DISNEY WORLD, ORLANDO, FLORIDA

There we were on the big steel bird flying toward Orlando. My favorite part of the flight was taking off, feeling the rush of the plane as it sped up and lifted into the air. I knew that my sister Denise, her husband Dick, and their kids Brittany and Brandon were already in Orlando waiting for us. My brother Andy and his wife Michele were on a flight behind us. Aunt Maureen, Uncle Denny, my cousin Michelle, and a friend of hers would come the next day.

We arrived in Orlando, and I was greeted by warm temperatures and a beautiful shining sun. I felt like nothing was wrong with me—I didn't feel any pain or discomfort, and I was determined to have a good time. We settled into our room at the Caribbean Beach Resort and began to relax. The atmosphere was pure gold—palm trees bigger than streetlights, Caribbean music playing in the background, and a pool that called my name.

Out by the pool, I started to feel uncomfortable, though. I knew my hat would have to come off, but I didn't have any hair. I thought, *What if people think I'm a boy? What if they stare?* After sitting there for a full five minutes watching everyone else have fun, I said, "The heck with it!" I didn't care what anyone else thought, and I certainly didn't need *hair* to have fun. I threw my towel aside and did a cannonball into the water.

Soon I was having the time of my life. I swam with Brittany and Brandon and had a blast. We rented little "water mouse boats" and went zipping around the lake and channel areas. We ate at the Old Port Royale food court, where Brittany and Brandon got kids' meals served in pails, complete with shovels.

Our days were filled with beaches, sand, and water. We went to Cocoa Beach, where my mom looked for seashells to take home. We also spent time at Clearwater Beach, where the warm water was as blue as the sky. One day, Andy and I went snorkeling and saw some really cool fish. I hoped to find sunken treasure but found only seashells instead.

THANKSGIVING DAY CAME FAST. Soon it was time to go back to Minnesota—back to reality, back to fighting cancer. Part of me wanted to stay in Florida forever. I had enjoyed being free from medical treatments and not having to think about what lay ahead of me. But we had to say good-bye to the warm weather in Florida and head back home, where the below-zero temperatures awaited us.

When we arrived in Albany, I tried not to think about what came next. The following morning, I would have to return to the hospital for my next round of chemo. I couldn't help but think about how, normally, I would dread going back to school after Thanksgiving break—but now, I would have gladly gone to school seven days a week if it meant not having to have cancer and do chemo.

On the night of Thanksgiving, I realized how many simple things I used to take for granted, like having hair, going to school, playing sports, and being able to hold down food. I guess it's human nature to take most of life for granted, but I was quickly learning to cherish even the smallest things. You just never know how suddenly it all can change.

UNIVERSITY OF MINNESOTA
CHILDREN'S HOSPITAL, FAIRVIEW

My fourth round of chemotherapy was to be a whole new
combination of drugs—a potent cocktail called ICE, which
stood for Ifosimide, Cytoxine, and Etoposide. The effects
on my body were expected to be much harsher because the
combination of meds used in the ICE regimen was known to
be more myelosuppressive, or harder on the marrow. As a
result, my counts would likely drop for longer periods of time,
and I would be more susceptible to infections and bleeding.

The doctors wanted me to move on to the ICE chemo for
a couple of reasons. First, a person can receive only so much
Adriamycin, a drug used in my previous chemo treatments,
because of the prolonged effects it may have on the body's
other organs. And second, by using different drugs, we were
hoping to outsmart the cancer. A cancerous tumor can find
ways to survive the drugs used to kill it, but the cancer has to
relearn how to survive in response to each new drug. Cancer
is smart—we just have to outsmart it (almost like a chess
game: outwit, outsmart, and survive).

The day before this round of chemo would start, I had to
meet with Dr. Cheng. My dad and Denise were with me, but
my mom had to stay home. Her job of running a daycare

wasn't as flexible as my dad's, so he was now in charge of getting me to my appointments. I knew that my mom wanted to come along on these visits, but it just wasn't possible.

With osteosarcoma, there generally comes a point in therapy known as "local control," where the tumor itself needs to be addressed. Because radiation therapy isn't a curative in osteosarcoma, surgical removal of the tumors is the standard care. Dr. Cheng reviewed my most recent scans and said that the tumor in my leg was shrinking but not very fast. The chemo was helping to reduce the tumor—as well as the pain in my leg—and I was happy about that. But we needed to discuss surgery.

That was when Dr. Cheng dropped a bomb on me. He said that in order to remove the entire tumor, he thought he would have to amputate my leg.

Dr. Cheng explained that when a tumor is removed, the goal is for there to be "negative margins" after surgery. The tumor is sent to a pathologist, who looks at it under a microscope to see if a rim of normal tissue exists around the tumor. This rim of normal tissue, or the negative margin, shows that no part of the tumor has been left behind. In my case, the tumor was too big and too high up in my right leg to get a negative margin. Dr. Cheng would amputate as a way to go for the cure, but I was devastated.

I thought, *I've done everything I've been told to do, and now I'm going to lose my leg?* I had come to terms with losing my hair, but I knew it would grow back—I couldn't grow another leg. I felt empty. I had reached the end of my rope. I asked Dr. Cheng if he was sure that nothing else could be done. He said that during surgery he would look to see if there was any possibility of saving my leg, but it wasn't something to count on.

The walls in the room seemed to close in on me. The air seemed to disappear.

I REMEMBER SAYING to my sister, "They have heart transplants, and lung transplants, and all kinds of different transplants—well, why not a leg transplant?" I knew it wasn't an option, but I wondered why it couldn't be. My sister told me she was even willing to donate her own bone and have them put it in me—anything to help save my leg. She just couldn't believe what was happening to me. I was so young, and I had so much life left to live; now it seemed fairly certain that I would have to live it without my right leg.

MY DAD WANTED a second opinion, and Dr. Cheng agreed that it was a good idea. The surgery to remove my tumor was put on hold, but I would need to do another round of ICE chemo treatment. Funny, I was suddenly relieved to do chemo.

My fourth round of chemo was really tough. The nausea was uncontrollable, and I felt miserable. The doctors and nurses did everything they could to help, but nothing seemed to work. I put up with the nausea and reminded myself again and again that I was fighting for my leg, fighting for my life.

MAYO CLINIC, ROCHESTER, MINNESOTA

My appointment at the Mayo Clinic was scheduled for a morning in late December, which meant finishing my chemo one day earlier than planned. Because of this, I had to drink my Mesna, a medication that's usually given through an IV. (The ICE cocktail could cause hemorrhagic cystitis, or bleeding in the bladder, and Mesna was a bladder protectant.) Today, not only did I have to drink the Mesna but I also had to do so *three* times and keep it down. My dad, my bucket, and I were off to Rochester, and it was a long and miserable ride.

The doctor at Mayo examined me, took down my history, and listened as we told him about my case. He felt positive about my situation and the possibility of saving my leg, although he said he couldn't be certain until he'd had a chance to look carefully at my scans. This was the best news I'd heard in a long time. It seemed that, at least for now, the odds were in my favor.

Days later, as I waited at home for the call from Mayo, I hoped and prayed for the news I wanted. The call finally came, but as soon as I got on the phone with the doctor, I knew the news wasn't good. He said he was sorry, but after reviewing the scans and talking with my doctors at Fairview, he realized that there was no way to save my leg. All my hopes were washed down the drain.

It would have been easy to give up, but I was in this fight for the long haul. I knew that I was being cared for by some of the top doctors in the country, and their decision to amputate my leg would help keep me alive. Facing the fact that I would live the rest of my life with one leg was terrifying, but I decided that if it would save my life then it was worth it. I told myself that someday having only one leg would seem normal to me. I had come this far and couldn't give up now. I was determined to move forward with full force.

Between now and the time of my surgery, I would need to have two more rounds of ICE chemotherapy. I hadn't been back to school since my first round of chemo. I missed seeing my friends every day and doing regular kid things. Still, I held onto hope.

Don't be afraid to get a second opinion.

Getting a second opinion is a smart thing to do, even when you trust the doctors who are most familiar with your case. Don't be afraid to speak up, ask questions, and be a part of your own health care. Believe that the doctors are on your side—they want what's best for you. During one of the worst times during my fight, my doctor said that I was going to lose my leg, and I couldn't live with just his word on the matter—I needed a second opinion. Even though it didn't turn out the way I'd hoped, I felt good about my decision to find out what another doctor had to say.

UNIVERSITY OF MINNESOTA
CHILDREN'S HOSPITAL, FAIRVIEW

I was going to lose my leg. I tried not to think about it because I was terrified. I had never felt fear like this before. Part of me didn't want to believe what was happening, but I knew that lying to myself would only make things worse.

In a strange sort of way, I actually felt fortunate that I knew ahead of time about losing my leg. The knowledge allowed me to prepare myself. On the other hand, I had more time to think about it—and having too much time to think isn't always such a good thing. I started to scare myself to the point that I wasn't sleeping at night. I didn't know how I was going to go on without my leg. I thought about how it might be for me to get around and how I would look. I couldn't imagine *what* I would look like. I knew I would look different, but I just couldn't picture myself in my mind's eye. Or maybe I just didn't want to.

ON MARCH 23, 2000, I had an appointment to see Dr. Cheng, the orthopedic surgeon. I wasn't looking forward to the visit because I would find out the date of my surgery—the date that marked the end of my life as I knew it.

Dr. Cheng wasn't my favorite person at that time. He

seemed insensitive, and he scared me with his words about what was going to happen. He seemed to act like it was normal to tell someone that she was going to lose her leg. I was only fourteen, though, and still trying to deal with the fact that I had cancer.

My sister, Denise, came along that day to give my dad and me some extra moral support. She had heard about Dr. Cheng and wanted to meet him in person. He specialized not only in surgery but also in the study of the survival and treatment of patients with soft tissue sarcomas. Every time I saw him, he wore a bowtie.

Despite all that was happening, Denise and I actually had fun in the car on the way down to the Twin Cities. We played games and didn't really talk about where we were going. Time passed quickly as we drove. The mood suddenly changed when we reached the hospital parking ramp.

We arrived at the clinic on time, ready to hear what had to be said. But we ended up having to wait an hour before we were called into a patient room. Another two hours passed, and still we waited.

I was so glad that my sister was there. She came to the rescue, turning the hours we waited into time when we could laugh and have some fun. She kept going up to the wall intercom to say, "Yes, I would like to order a cheeseburger, fries, and a large Coke to go, please." She didn't really push the button, of course.

Then she dug through her purse and found some crayons. We started to color on the big sheet of paper that covered the examination table. Soon it became a masterpiece, as we drew a nature scene with trees, birds, and a beautiful sun. We also played a few games of Tic-Tac-Toe and ordered some more burgers off the intercom.

Finally, Dr. Cheng appeared. It was a short visit compared

to the wait. He said my surgery was scheduled for March 28, only five days away. My mind suddenly became crowded with thoughts. I would have to do every active thing I could in those few days before surgery.

Both my sister and dad were there to support me if I needed it, but I stayed strong. I had been preparing myself for weeks. As we left the hospital for home, I didn't want to be sad and dwell on my situation. I didn't want to sit and think about how scared I really was.

ALBANY, MINNESOTA

In the days leading up to my surgery, I did everything I could think of using my two legs for the last time. I played basket-ball, rode my bike, went Rollerblading, and ran around for no reason at all. It was hard for me to do these activities because I was exhausted from my last chemo treatment. I wanted to do even more, and it made me angry that I couldn't. And yet, I was grateful that I was able to do what I did.

I spent lots of time with my family and went shopping with my friends. I wanted to be able to walk through the mall one last time.

One night, I told my closest friends, Catherine and Savannah, that I needed to have my leg amputated because of the cancer. Telling them was hard, but I'd made my peace with losing my leg. They were shocked, but they told me that everything would be okay. I let them know that I would be really weak for a while after the surgery and wouldn't be able to do all of the stuff we usually did. They understood and said that they'd always be there for me.

The days went by so fast, kind of like vacation days. Before I knew it, March 27 arrived—only one more day until my surgery.

That night, I made a memory of my leg. I watched my leg as it moved, and I took extra notice when I walked. I sat with my legs crossed, and then sat on the floor pretzel style. I wanted to remember my leg, and this was my way of doing it. I even slept on my right side so I could feel my right leg beneath me one final time.

Deep inside, I still hoped the doctors would discover that the tumor in my leg wasn't as big and bad as they thought. I hoped they would be able to save my leg somehow. It was a one-in-a-million chance, but I held onto it. That was the only way I could get through the waking hours leading up to the surgery.

UNIVERSITY OF MINNESOTA
CHILDREN'S HOSPITAL, FAIRVIEW

On March 28, I was admitted to the hospital for the amputation of my right leg, as scheduled. My mom, dad, and Denise were with me. When we arrived, Chris, the child family life specialist, brought me to have a special molding taken of my right foot so I could remember it.

Denise came with me for the molding. Chris gave me a bucket that I was supposed to put my right foot into while she poured the cold molding material over it. I had to hold my foot still for ten minutes before I was allowed to move. I couldn't even squish my toes around, though it was tempting.

I sat and thought about how this would be the last time I'd ever do anything with my right foot. My foot wouldn't be there in a few hours. I was glad my sister was with me, because she always made me feel calmer. After the impression of my foot had been made, Chris took us to meet up with our parents in the surgery waiting area.

Of course, the one time when I could have waited forever, a pre-op room became available right away. I had to leave my family behind as I went through the pre-op procedures of getting my weight, blood pressure, and oxygen levels checked. In the pre-op room, I felt my breathing grow heavy and I began to panic. I didn't want to be there. I didn't want this to be happening. I wanted out. Inside I screamed with fear, but I tried hard not to show it. I told myself to be strong for my mom and dad.

Soon my parents and sister were able to join me again. We sat together quietly; no one really knew what to say. Denise, who normally tried to lighten the mood, was suddenly serious. She told me that things were going to be different for me after the surgery but, together as a family, we could get through this. My family tried to reassure me that it wouldn't matter what I looked like afterward—they just wanted me with them and would always love me, no matter what. Tears filled my eyes.

I knew everything would be different when I woke up— once I closed my eyes that day, I would open them to a world that had been forever changed. As it got closer to the time of the surgery, I felt overwhelmed. I got nauseated and thought I was going to throw up. One of the nurses gave me some medication to help me relax. After that, I felt a little sleepy and less anxious. I lay there crying on the inside. More than anything, I just wanted to go home.

THE SURGICAL NURSES were ready for me in the operating room. My mom, my dad, and my sister hugged and kissed me and said they would be there when I woke up. They told me they loved me very much. As I was wheeled away from my family down the cold hallway, I felt the jab of every bump. In the OR, I was given more medication, and the lights above blurred. I slowly drifted further and further away.

Before the surgery, my dad and brother had asked Dr. Cheng if it might be possible to save the lower half of my leg, which was still healthy, and to connect that bone and muscle to my hip so I could have a partial leg. Their hope was that it would then be easier for me to use a prosthetic leg. Dr. Cheng *was* able to save my tibia, or lower leg bone, and connect it to my hip with rods and pins.

The surgery took six hours to complete. While I was in the OR, other family members including my brother Andy showed up to keep my mom, dad, and sister company. The doctors periodically updated everyone about the surgery and how I was doing.

AS I LAY ON THE TABLE in the OR, one of the doctors said, "Amy, Amy, can you hear me?" I woke up and immediately tried to wiggle the toes on my right foot, but they didn't move. My leg was gone.

It hurt so badly—a pain that seemed a thousand times worse than any physical pain I had ever known. I was given morphine, and I fell in and out of sleep. I don't recall much of what happened that night, but I do remember going up to my room on 5B. It was late, and everyone came in to say goodnight and then left. I was alone.

Stay strong.

I had to be strong before and after my surgery, not only physically but emotionally, too. I had to get used to how people stared. It's okay not to like the way people see you—it only matters how you see yourself. I learned to accept the way other people viewed me, and I learned to like me for *me*. I was who I was: a strong person I loved and who wanted to live.

5B, PEDIATRIC ONCOLOGY FLOOR, UNIVERSITY OF MINNESOTA CHILDREN'S HOSPITAL

The next few days were a tremendous challenge. My first difficulty was getting out of bed. My amputated leg, which I nicknamed "Shorty," hurt too much to bend. The muscles hadn't loosened up since the surgery. To get out of bed, I had to roll over to my side first and then push myself up with my arms. It was hard, but eventually I got the hang of it.

I also had to learn how to use crutches, which would now be my way around. The physical therapist told me that walking on crutches took arm strength. She said most people think you use your armpits to get around on crutches, but you shouldn't—it's all in the arms. I started out by swinging my body forward and following with my crutches as soon as I put my left foot on the ground. The therapist told me it would be easy once I got the hang of it, and she was right.

Every day, I practiced walking on crutches with a physical therapist. We took our daily stroll down the hall of 5B, around the nurses' station, and around the 5A side of the floor. At first, I had to take a lot of breaks. But as I regained some of my strength, walking on crutches got easier.

I worked with an occupational therapist to learn how to bathe, get dressed, and do other daily tasks. Because Shorty was covered with bandages and drains after the surgery, I couldn't take a bath or shower—I had to take sponge baths instead. (Plus, I couldn't even stand up long enough to take a shower.) The drains on Shorty were there to get rid of the excess blood and fluid, so I wouldn't get an infection. I knew I was stitched and stapled all down my right side, and I was okay with that. I wasn't ready to see what was left of my leg yet.

I had a catheter in for the first few days after my amputation, so I wouldn't have to get up to use the bathroom. When they finally took the catheter out, it made for some interesting times. It was still very painful to bend Shorty. I had to somehow stand over the toilet to go, but once my pain was more under control, I figured it out. Something as simple as putting a sock on my left foot was also difficult. I would be in too much pain to move, but I knew that if I wanted to get better, I was going to have to be strong and just do it.

I learned exercises designed to help me regain my leg strength. One of the exercises was as basic as lifting Shorty up. While lying down, I had to keep a bag of powdered sugar on top of Shorty to help loosen up the muscles. These tasks may sound simple, but they were very difficult in the beginning. At times, I cried and screamed into my pillow, but this did nothing to relieve my anger, frustration, and fear.

The strangest thing after my amputation was a feeling I had in my amputated leg known as "phantom pain." After losing a limb, you may sometimes get the sensation that the limb is still there and can feel pain. Sometimes, I'd feel an itch on my right leg, the one that had been amputated. I would then scratch my left leg in the same spot, which seemed to help.

I WOULD NEVER want to relive the first few days after my surgery. The only thing that got me through that time was my determination to win my battle. Everything I endured before, during, and after the amputation helped me learn to be stronger. Still, there were times when it felt as if my world had fallen apart.

One night during my recovery, I called my mom and dad at home in tears, asking them to come down and stay with me. It was nine thirty, and I wanted them to come right then, even though I knew it wasn't possible. Both of my parents had to work the next day and the drive to the hospital took hours. They said that I would probably be asleep by the time they got there and that the nurses could help me. This wasn't the answer I wanted to hear.

My mom knew what to do. She called the nurses' station and one of the nurses, Crista, came to my room and stayed with me. She sat and cried with me as I spilled my guts to her. Everything that I had kept bottled up inside exploded from me. I told her that I hated having only one leg, that every move I made took such a huge effort. I told her I still couldn't even go to the bathroom without a struggle. She said that, in time, things would get easier, that I would heal and feel whole again. She promised me I'd get through it and said it was okay to ask for help; asking didn't mean I was weak.

I really needed to hear someone say that. Before, I had never called the nurses to help me go to the bathroom or reach something because I didn't want to admit that I needed help. Thanks to Crista, I got through my first post-op breakdown, and I was so grateful to her. That night, she sat in my room until I finally fell asleep.

NOT LONG AFTER my surgery, I went outside on a sunny day and saw my shadow for the first time after my amputation. I stood there with my parents, thinking that I didn't look complete, that something was missing. Suddenly, it sunk in— I didn't have a right leg anymore. I wanted my leg to be there in the shadow, but it was gone and would never be there again. The realization hit me hard. I knew at that moment how I looked—who I was—and I had to accept it.

Talk about your feelings.

It's okay to voice your frustrations and fear. Tell someone what you're thinking and how you feel. If you're facing surgery, have confidence in the surgeons; they know what they're doing. Trust your doctors, nurses, and therapists. Talk to them about any concerns you have; let people know how you feel. Tell your family about what you're going through, instead of trying to protect them. It's okay to be sad or angry or scared. It's okay to need help. Believe in your heart of hearts that things will get better—that *you* will get better.

ALBANY, MINNESOTA

In the safety of the hospital, I had started getting used to having only one leg, but the outside world was a different story. I returned home, and life was anything but normal. At first, it was hard for me to go out in public because I was afraid people would stare.

One Saturday morning, my parents and I went to do our usual weekend errands. I knew this would be uncomfortable for me, but I understood that I had to toughen up and accept how people reacted. We went to the mall to shop and look around. I rode in a wheelchair because I wasn't yet strong enough to get around the mall on crutches. I didn't like riding in the wheelchair—it seemed to invite more stares.

As soon as we walked through the doors of the mall, I felt as if all eyes were on me. People had stared when I lost my hair and wore a hat, but I figured they were probably trying to figure out whether I was a boy or a girl. But now, they really stared and probably knew there was something wrong with me. I told myself that these people didn't know I had cancer and weren't used to seeing a person with one leg. The smart ones and the ones who cared probably figured out that I had a life-threatening disease.

I didn't like being stared at, but at least I hadn't lost my touch for shopping. Soon, all of our shopping bags were hanging off the sides of my wheelchair so we didn't have to carry them. I thought, *Maybe they're staring because I look like a human shopping cart.*

What bugged me most was that some people stared just to stare. They had no idea what my life was like, what I had been through, or why I had one leg. Adults who stared really made me angry. I wanted to go up to them and say, "Yes, I have one leg." What were they waiting for—I mean, did they think that if they stared long enough my leg would magically reappear?

I understood when children stared, because they were naturally curious. At my mom's daycare, some of the kids asked me questions like, "What happened to your leg?" and "Will your leg ever grow back?" I answered their questions the best way I could, and I was glad that the kids weren't afraid of me. I told them it was okay to ask me questions and that lots of other people in the world had only one leg. I even got used to going out in public and hearing some children exclaim, "Look, that boy only has one leg!" Needless to say, I was pretty excited whenever I heard, "Hey, look, that girl only has one leg!"

Still, there were times when having one leg left me feeling like less of a person, so I started to look at myself in the mirror and say, "It's not what's on the outside that counts, it's what's on the inside." After all, when they took my leg, they didn't take away my heart, my sense of humor, or my compassion for others.

THE FIRST TIME I saw my friends after my surgery, I was really nervous. I didn't know how they were going to react. I should have known that they wouldn't care how I looked. We were friends because we were friends, not because of how many legs I had. They asked me if I was still in pain and whether I was going to be able to get a prosthetic leg. I answered yes to both questions. After that, we had one of our usual fun nights of talking, watching movies, and eating junk food.

The things I used to stress about—like homework—didn't bother me as much anymore. Whenever I started to get wound up about something, I'd say to myself, "Is this as bad as losing a leg?" Of course, the answer was always no. Life had definitely changed for me, but I just tried to keep it all in perspective.

Every day, I grew stronger. I understood more and more that what's on the inside matters more than what's on the outside. I leaned on my family and friends for support, and they leaned on me. They were all I needed to make it in this world.

UNIVERSITY OF MINNESOTA
CHILDREN'S HOSPITAL, FAIRVIEW

It was spring, and the sun had melted the Minnesota winter away. I was in the middle of my fight, halfway through the protocol prescribed by Dr. Neglia. I had been treated with six rounds of chemotherapy and had six more to go.

Now it was time to address the small tumors in my lungs. They had to come out, whether I was ready or not.

I was scheduled to have surgery on my right lung in May. At the same time, I would get a new port, a double one. I'd had a single port since the beginning, and now the doctors wanted to put in a double, which meant two needles could administer medications at one time. With the single port, the nurses had to wait for one medicine to be finished before they could give the next dose. A double port would save everyone some time.

ON THE DAY of my surgery, I was taken down to the pre-op room in the early morning. My dad was with me. I had gotten a nice send-off from the nurses as I was wheeled past their desk. Crista and another nurse named Jill had walked me down the hall to the elevators to make sure that I was safely on my way.

The OR nurses did all the usual pre-op tasks, and when they were done, my dad came to sit with me. "Here we go again," he said.

Dr. Leonard, the pediatric thoracic surgeon who would do the thoracotomy, came in and explained the procedure. He said that they would make a nine-inch incision under my right armpit, and then remove one of my ribs to gain access to my lung. They would then deflate my lung so Dr. Leonard could work his magic. He would use his hands to feel my lung and find the nodules. I had heard that Dr. Leonard could feel something as tiny as a grain of sand, so I was confident that he would do a good job.

As he explained the procedure, I thought about how weird it was that his hand would actually touch my lung. I was scared, but he reassured me that everything would be okay. He said he'd performed the procedure thousands of times. After hearing that, I felt better.

Next, it was time for the medication that would help me sleep. At this point, I didn't mind it because it was the one thing that kept me calm enough to go into the operating room. As I was rolled down the hall, I felt more alert than I had for my leg amputation. I even saw the OR, with its bright lights and shiny knives and clamps. Everyone in the OR tried to make me as comfortable as possible.

I felt them move me onto the operating table and start connecting me to machines. The anesthesiologist put a mask over my face, told me to take some deep breaths, and asked if I was getting sleepy. I wasn't, so I told him to turn it up a notch because no one was going to put his hand on my lung while I was awake! He gave me a smile. My eyelids got heavier and heavier, and then I was out.

DURING MY SURGERY, Dr. Cheng came and did some re-grafting on Shorty, where some of the dead skin had turned black. So, not only did I have the lung nodules taken out, but I also got a new port and had some work done on my leg. I was like a car getting an overhaul, new parts, and a tune-up.

When I woke up in the recovery room afterward, I felt intense pain on my right side, as if needles were poking me all over. The doctors had placed a tube in my side to suck out all the excess fluid in my lung. The tube felt uncomfortable, and I wanted it out. The nurses gave me morphine. As I lay there in pain, I thought, *Will this ever end?*

I was taken to my room on 5B where I could rest. My main doctor, Dr. Neglia, came to visit me. He said that Dr. Leonard had taken out seven nodules and one rib. Dr. Leonard and Dr. Cheng were both pleased with how the surgery had gone. However, I learned that starting now Shorty would need to be cleaned out every other day, which meant more trips to the OR.

The following morning, I tried to move my right arm but couldn't. I pushed the call button so a nurse would come. I was scared because no one had mentioned that I might not be able to move my arm. I was even more scared when the nurse had to get the doctor to come and take a look. By the time the doctor got there, I was in a panic, but he reassured me that the movement in my arm would return in time. He explained that the surgeons had cut through muscles and small nerves; it would take a while for my arm to heal.

The next day, I had to go back to the OR for Shorty's first cleaning. The drill was familiar to me: go to pre-op, check in, get my sleepy medication, lights out. Afterward, I returned to my room and slept for hours.

MY HOSPITAL STAY was long, and there wasn't much for me to do. Because I spent so much time there, I had started referring to the hospital as "The Fairview Inn."

To pass the time, I'd go down to the nurses' station for a visit or watch a movie. On Tuesdays and Thursdays, I watched the hospital channel, which produced shows like "The TV Show" and "The Game Show," where patients participated and could win prizes. I loved those two shows and made sure to tell my family not to call me when they were on. My sister Denise always forgot, though, and I'd make her call me back later.

As the days dragged on, I started to think about what I was missing at home and school. I knew I'd missed some school dances and the spring fling, where everyone got out of school and could hang out and have fun with their friends. I wasn't having any fun. I was frustrated, and to make matters worse, I still couldn't move my arm. I wondered if the doctor had been wrong when he'd told me I'd be able to move it again. This thought really scared me.

I began to slip into a depression. I didn't eat well, and I never felt happy. The nurses noticed; they took extra time each day to visit with me and started me on a supplemental drink to help increase my calorie intake.

By day seven, I could move my fingers. That was a relief. And by day ten, almost all of the movement in my arm had returned. This helped me to feel a lot more comfortable, but the best medicine for me was the knowledge that I was going home. My ten-day stay was over. I'd get to spend time in Albany for a few days before my second thoracotomy.

THOSE FIVE DAYS in between hospital visits were frustrating. Because I was still healing from lung surgery, I couldn't use my crutches—the pain on my side was too much. I had to use a wheelchair, but that was frustrating too because the doorways at home weren't wide enough for it. I was determined to get to the point where I could use my crutches and, sure enough, I was using them two days before I was due back at Fairview.

To prepare for my surgery, I had to give myself antibiotics at home. The antibiotics would help prevent Shorty from getting infected. Any kind of infection would have been a setback at that point, so I learned how to take care of myself.

Five days later, I was back at the hospital for another thoracotomy, this time on my left side. The operation went smoothly, as planned. During the surgery, Dr. Cheng checked Shorty again and everything looked good.

I was so happy after the surgery. I had known what to expect because I'd been through it once before. I told myself that everything would be okay—it would be easy. I think it was my positive attitude that helped me to recover quickly and get released from the hospital in a record three days.

I thought I was finally back on track. But three weeks later, all of my physical strength, emotional resilience, and mental determination were put to the test once again.

Stay determined to fight.

Cancer is more than tumors and chemo—it's like a fight against evil. I was scared and worried half the time I was going through treatment because I never knew what each day was going to bring, but one thing was for sure: I knew I had to face my situation with determination. It was my will to live each day, even the bad days. I wouldn't give up. I couldn't let cancer win.

5B, PEDIATRIC ONCOLOGY FLOOR, UNIVERSITY OF MINNESOTA CHILDREN'S HOSPITAL

During the next round of ICE chemo, I experienced the usual sleeping, puking, and puking some more. But one morning while I was at home, I spiked a really high fever and had chills. I drank cold water to help cool my body down. But I was hot to the touch, and I could feel the heat coming off my head. I knew the situation was serious.

The homecare nurse who had come to check on me said, "You don't look so good." She immediately called Jody, the pediatric nurse practitioner at Fairview, who said, "Put her in a car and get her here as soon as possible." I called my dad at work, and he returned home right away to take me to the hospital in Minneapolis.

After I was admitted to the hospital, I was immediately given an isolation room and put on a combination of antibiotics to fight infection. The doctors ran tests to find out what was wrong. They drew blood and took cultures to be tested in the lab. The doctors needed to find out the exact type of infection I had, so they'd know which antibiotics would best work.

The nurses hooked me up to IV fluids, and I drank water like crazy to cool down. I knew I looked as bad as I felt; my face was pale, and I lay in bed shivering. When the doctor on call and the resident came to see me, they joked around, asking me, "Are you sick? You look sick!" For me, humor was good medicine.

The rest of the day, the nurses came in and out of my room as I slept, but with all the fluids I was getting, sleep came in small doses; I had to get up every half hour to go to the bathroom. I got to the point of holding it to see how much I could actually pee at one time.

The next day, I started to feel better. I was well enough to play a few hands of Cribbage (a card game) with the nurses and residents. At this point, I didn't need my family to stay with me at the hospital. I had grown comfortable with the surroundings, and the nurses had become friends I looked forward to seeing at every visit. I actually began to welcome my alone time at the hospital.

IT WAS NOW JUNE, and by this time, my medical expenses were adding up fast. A group of very dedicated people organized a benefit dinner and silent auction in my honor to raise funds to put toward my medical expenses. The dinner was scheduled for the evening of June 22.

I was excited about the menu of spaghetti, salad, garlic bread, and dessert. I just couldn't believe that almost everyone I knew had pitched in to help. A bunch of caring people had donated some wonderful items for the auction. There was only one problem with the event. I was in the hospital with a raging fever.

I wanted to attend the benefit so badly, and I knew I would need to convince the doctors to let me go. I begged and whined until I got my way. The doctors agreed to let me attend, on two conditions: the first was to drink lots of fluids, and the second was to be back in time for my next round of meds. My nurse Carolyn planned to come along to help me out and to make sure I was in good hands if anything should happen.

The benefit was to be held in the basement of the Church of St. Benedict in Avon, a town near Albany. That night, both Carolyn and my brother Andy, along with his wife Michele, escorted me to the big gala. I drank plenty of fluids on the way there (in fact, I drank so much that I knew my first stop had to be the bathroom).

As we drove up to the church, I saw a lot of parked cars but I wasn't prepared for what was inside. A sea of people awaited me: family, friends, neighbors, almost the entire community, including many people I didn't know. I was speechless at first. I was shocked and overwhelmed by the amount of people who were there to support me.

I talked to everyone I could. They all told me that I was doing a great job, that I should keep fighting, and that they were happy to be of help. Their words filled my heart with hope and love. Altogether, more than one thousand people showed up, which amazed me.

Later that night, I said good-bye to all my friends and family. Then Carolyn, my brother, his wife, and I left the benefit to head back to the hospital. After I returned to my room on 5B, the nurses hooked me back up to my IVs. I gave my brother a hug for all he'd done that night, and then we said good-bye.

The event had tired me out, and sleep came easily. I slept the next day away. The nurses knew that I was tired so they put a sign on my door saying "Shh . . . Sleeping."

THE DAYS PASSED, and I noticed that little spots had started to develop on Shorty. The doctors kept a close eye on the spots, not knowing what they were. I passed the time chatting with Jody, looking at magazines, and talking with the nurses at the desk.

Within a few days, the spots had increased. On day nine,

the doctor on call came to talk to me about what might be growing on Shorty: a fungus. I thought, *Fungus? Yuck!* By day ten, one of the spots had seeped enough that the doctors could take a culture of it and find out what it really was. True to the doctor's worst fears, the culture showed that I had a rapidly moving fungus.

The situation was serious, and I had to start a course of antibiotics. Not only did I have a fungus but my counts (mainly my white blood cell count and neutrophils) were also very low. In other words, my body didn't have enough defenses to fight off the fungus. The doctors didn't want the fungus to spread throughout my bloodstream, so I was put on amphotericineB, a very strong antibiotic. Little did I know then that I'd end up being on that antibiotic for five months.

By this stage in the game, the smaller spots had turned into four bigger spots, each about the size of a silver dollar. On day twelve of this latest development, I knew that the antibiotics were working because during the night when I got up to go to the bathroom, I felt something fall. When I turned on the light and saw what had happened, I freaked out. Something gross had fallen out of Shorty.

I panicked and called Elisa, my nurse. When she got to my room, I said, "What *is* this, and why is it on the floor?" She looked at the floor, then at me, and finally at Shorty. There was a big hole on Shorty, and I almost wanted to puke. Elisa picked the thing up from the floor with a pair of gloves and put it in a sterile container. I was a little shaken up, but Elisa calmed me down, telling me that I was fine and they would fix everything. She stuffed the hole in Shorty with gauze and told me to go back to sleep because there was nothing that could be done about the situation until morning.

The next morning when the doctors came in, they were pleased. They said that the antibiotics were working and the fungus had fallen out because it was dying. "Okay," I said and continued to trust them. I knew they had my best interest in mind.

A few more days passed with little excitement, but on day seventeen, Dr. Cheng came to my room and told me that I had to have more surgery. He said that he needed to remove the rest of the fungus spots. I had mixed feelings about this. On the one hand, I would have to go through surgery again, which I wasn't a big fan of; on the other hand, I'd be rid of the disgusting fungus. I agreed to the plan, and my surgery was set for the next day.

I WAS "NPO" the night before my surgery, which meant that I couldn't eat or drink anything. This didn't bother me because I wasn't in the mood to eat anyway. My mom and my sister Denise came to support me the morning of the surgery. I was calm, knowing this operation would be simpler than the others I'd been through.

A few hours passed, and we began to wonder why I hadn't been taken down to pre-op yet. When my nurse came in, she told me that our spot in the OR was taken and I wouldn't be able to go in until sometime later that day. My mom, Denise, and I talked and played games. As time wore on, I started to get thirsty. I still wasn't allowed to eat or drink because we didn't know when I was going into the OR.

By dinnertime, I was totally frustrated. My mom and sister weren't too happy either, but there was nothing we could do. Late that night, I was finally taken to the OR to have my procedure done. I'd waited so long, but the surgery itself only took an hour or so. Dr. Cheng was able to remove the fungus successfully and stuff the holes with gauze.

It was well into the early morning hours when I returned to my room. My sister had gone home already, but my mom had stayed and I was glad she was there when I woke. Shorty was covered with an Ace wrap, and the dressing didn't have to be changed for two days, so things were good. At this point, though, I was sick of the hospital and wanted to go home.

Two days after my surgery, my pain tolerance was really put to the test. The time had come for the nurses to unwrap Shorty and change the bandages. At first, it felt good to have the Ace wrap removed, but when the nurses started to pull on the gauze, pain ripped up and down my spine. I completely lost it. Everyone tried to calm me down, but nothing worked.

They drenched the sticky gauze with saline, but it still felt as if every little blood vessel and nerve ending was pulled as the nurses tugged the gauze. My wounds broke open, and I screamed out in pain. I wanted them to stop—I wanted all of this to be over—but I knew I had to go on.

I was given morphine to take the edge off, but even that didn't help. I was in the worst pain of my life. My mom stayed by my side the whole time; it was a nightmare for her. All she could do was sit there and hold my hand. That was the longest half hour of my life, but my mom and I got through it. The nurses put new gauze on the holes and rewrapped Shorty. I dreaded the next change of dressing later that day.

Chris, the child family life specialist, came to talk to me and help me get through the pain of the next changing. She massaged my foot, which took some of my pain away. She told me to concentrate on my "happy place," which was Walt Disney World, and she played soft music in the background. Chris told me that when my dressings were changed, I should go to my happy place and concentrate really hard on that. It helped to a point. I still felt the pain, but I was able to control myself.

For the first week after surgery, my bandages were changed three times a day, and then two times a day after that. I needed morphine every time. I spent another week in the hospital and had lots of family and friends come to visit.

My immune system built itself up and, after a while, I was able to handle the dressing changes without morphine. After a total of twenty-eight days in the hospital, I was finally released. I was so ready to leave.

My bags were packed, and my dad came to pick me up. All I could think of was that I was leaving and not coming back—well, not until the next chemo anyway.

You are stronger than you know.

The long, trying days I spent in the hospital taught me about strength I never knew I had, both physical and emotional. Cancer continued to teach me many things about myself, including how much pain I could tolerate, how much stress I could take, and how far I could push myself when necessary. I wouldn't have known these things if I hadn't gotten sick, and I had to grow up fast. It's true that cancer presents you with challenges you don't want, but, to survive, you've got to face those challenges head on.

ALBANY, MINNESOTA

Four months had passed since the infection in Shorty, and I had finished six more rounds of chemo. By this point, chemo had become routine for me, and I felt stronger than ever, both physically and mentally. After thirteen total months of hard work, pushing myself to limits I never knew existed, I was *done*.

On December 1, 2000, I left the hospital with my dad. That day already meant a lot to me because it was the day my Grandma Rose had died the year I was in the fourth grade. As I left Fairview, I felt that she was watching over me.

When I got home, I was so happy to see my mom. She gave me a huge hug and said that I had done what I had to do and had done it with pride. I felt all tingly inside when she said that. I thought that my fight was finally over and my life could go back to normal, whatever normal was now.

As the days passed, I grew stronger. I worked with a tutor, spent time with friends, and went to see my niece Brittany and my nephew Brandon at their sporting events. I knew that in January, I'd need to go back to the hospital for a bone scan, chest CT, and other tests. Until then, I would enjoy each moment.

THE MEDICAL TESTS were performed as scheduled, and that same day we went to see Dr. Neglia to find out the results. My dad and I sat in the familiar plain white patient room. My heart pounded, beads of sweat gathered on my forehead, and I sat there hoping and praying for good news. My dad kept his cool. He and I didn't talk much because we were thinking about what the doctor might say.

Dr. Neglia walked into the room, and the first thing he said was, "The scans are all good." I swallowed, and my heart finally slowed in my chest. The weight had been lifted.

After talking to us some more, Dr. Neglia said, "Well, we'll see you in three months." I went to tell all the nurses on 5B. In the car, I called everyone I could think of to share the news. I felt like I could finally go back to being a regular kid.

SOON, I RETURNED to school, after having missed a whole year. I was nervous and excited. Everyone welcomed me back. My friends and teachers helped me to catch up. In time, I fell back into the routine of school. I loved it. For the first time in a long time, I felt normal again.

Another three months passed before I had to return to the hospital for more scans. That day in April, I had a bone scan and chest CT, and had X-rays taken of Shorty. Between tests, I went to visit my favorite nurses on 5B. I hugged the first one I saw—I was so glad to see everyone.

When I saw Dr. Neglia, I gave him a big hug, too. I was grateful to him for having taken such good care of me and for always helping me feel at ease. To me, he had become like family, and I'd even started to refer to him as "Uncle Joe." I had often told him that he couldn't ever move to a different hospital or I would have to go along.

During this appointment, he checked me over and said that everything looked good. He said that I should schedule an appointment to see Dr. Cheng so he could look at the X-rays of Shorty. Dr. Neglia hadn't yet had the chance to analyze my scans, but he gave me a clean bill of health and told us to return in another three months.

My dad and I arrived home in the late afternoon, and I got out my unfinished homework. The phone rang at five fifteen.

My dad answered, and I could tell right away by the sound of his voice that something was terribly wrong. My heart dropped into my stomach. I sat motionless. Chills ran through my body.

After he'd hung up, my dad asked my mom and me to come to the dining room table. He told us that my chest CT scan showed two spots on my right and left lungs. I put my head down on the table and started to cry. Why, after I had done my job with the chemo, did the cancer have to come back? I was crushed. Both my mom and dad gave me a hug and said that I'd be able to do it again.

I went to my room and sat there in disbelief. I was so angry at the cancer—how could it have come back? I wanted to reach into my body and rip the cancer out. I wanted to slam it on the ground and stomp on it with my foot.

I knew I had to tell my brother and sister. I called Andy first, but I couldn't even say hi without crying. He said, "What's the matter?" All I could get out was, "It's back." He knew instantly what I meant. Andy tried to tell me I'd be okay, that I was strong enough to keep fighting. Then he said, "Hey, you'll be able to get your sleepy medicine again," and I had to chuckle at that. He knew how to make me see the lighter side of life.

Next, I called Denise. I started sobbing before she had even picked up the phone. When she heard me crying, she knew exactly what was wrong. She told me that she'd had an uncomfortable feeling the whole day and sensed that something was going to happen. The first thing she asked was, "Where is it?" I told her the cancer was in my lungs, and she was just as scared, angry, and frustrated as I was. But she lifted me up with some encouraging words. She said that our family would get me through whatever came next.

The following day, Jody called from Fairview to tell us that my surgery was set for April 18. She said the doctors would start with my left lung. Life had changed so fast again.

UNIVERSITY OF MINNESOTA
CHILDREN'S HOSPITAL, FAIRVIEW

My nerves were on edge. We were at the hospital early, and this time my mom had come along with my dad and me. I was glad she was there to keep us company. My surgery was delayed two hours, and when I finally was taken into the pre-op room, the routine felt familiar to me. I took medication to help me sleep, and I drifted off, waving good-bye to my parents.

Afterward, I was brought up to my room on 5B. I lay there, concentrating on breathing, which was hard to do because I had a chest tube sticking out of my left side. My family and relatives came to visit me, and they all had big smiles for me every time I managed to open my eyes. My nephew Brandon held my hand.

Two days after my surgery, it was time for the chest tube to come out. The doctors who removed the tube weren't very gentle. They ripped the tape off of my already tender skin. As they pulled the tube out, I could feel it rubbing against my ribs.

Dr. Jeff, one of the medical residents, took good care of me after my surgery and often came in to chat about the day when he could. I complained to Dr. Jeff about the rough tape pulling, and he said, "Okay, then you can put a piece of tape on me and pull it off."

So I found the stickiest tape ever and put it on the hairiest part of Dr. Jeff's arm. My nurse Amy and Dr. Jeff laughed as I played doctor. I was nice and pulled the tape off his arm quickly—I could have done it slower and inflicted more pain, but I didn't. It was a fun moment. I had known Dr. Jeff since he was a medical student, and he was one of my favorite people at the hospital.

Look on the bright side.

Cancer is scary, and hospitals aren't the most fun places in the world, but it's okay to have a good time when you can and to have a positive outlook. During long hospital stays, I figured, "Why not try and have some fun?" I enjoyed talking with the nurses, playing Cribbage with anyone I could corner, or hanging out with other kids who had cancer. One of my friends at the hospital was Heather, who had a brain tumor. She loved to joke around and goof off. Little Joey, or "Fuzzy-head," as many of us affectionately called him, was a fighter who always had a smile on his face. Jill was a girl close to my age who always had the best tips on passing time in the hospital (like raising your hospital bed up as high as it goes, having a bowl of ice cream and a bowl of popcorn, and then watching a movie). I didn't want the hospital to be a bad place, so I tried to think of it in a positive way. That helped make each visit a little better.

ORLANDO, FLORIDA

After the surgery, I took it easy at home and worked on regaining my strength. I had a good reason to get better quickly: I had been offered an opportunity to go back to Orlando, this time by the Make-A-Wish Foundation, which granted wishes to children with life-threatening medical conditions. My parents and I had the chance for a Disney Cruise vacation in May, and I had no intention of missing it. My sister and her family planned to come along, too. Denise had said that when I was done with this nightmare called cancer, we would go to my "happy place" again. It was a promise made between sisters.

During those weeks before our cruise, my world was filled with the anticipation of sunshine, dolphins, and all things Disney. I looked forward to leaving reality and my medical worries behind me.

Although my family worried about my health and whether we could make the trip, we were soon on our way. We arrived in sunny Orlando and took a Disney Cruise Line bus to Disney's Boardwalk Inn Resort. Denise and her family had arrived the day before and were waiting for us. The weather was gorgeous, the hotel was fabulous, and the company was the best.

I think the vacation gave me an extra boost of energy because I definitely didn't miss out on anything. For three days, we went to the amusement parks and I got to go on some of my favorite rides: Splash Mountain, Space Mountain, Tower of Terror, and more. We saw Disney shows like *Tarzan* and *The Lion King*. We ate at Cinderella's Castle in the Magic Kingdom. We even went to Epcot Center, where we visited the Biergarten, a German restaurant; Denise's husband Dick was in seventh heaven because he got to drink a lot of beer. It was amazing to me that just a few weeks earlier I'd had surgery, and now I was vacationing with my family in my favorite place in the world.

WHEN IT WAS TIME to finally board the *Disney Wonder* cruise ship, I could barely contain my excitement. The ship entrance was shaped like Mickey Mouse's head. It was the most beautiful ship I'd ever seen. Our stateroom had a veranda, and I looked forward to standing on it during sunset and trying to catch a glimpse of dolphins in the Caribbean Sea below.

Soon we were headed for the beautiful islands of the Bahamas. We dined at Triton's, the ship restaurant with an under-the-sea theme. Afterward, we went to see a show in the Walt Disney Theater. As we sat and watched the show that first night, the seas grew rough and the ship started to rock. My mom and I felt queasy, and later that night Denise left our stateroom to get us all something to help with the nausea. By the time she got back, my mom was in the bathroom and I was throwing up in a wastebasket. Here I was on vacation, and I was puking—and not from chemo this time! The waters were so rough that we could hear other people's closet doors sliding and slamming as the ship rocked. The first night was the worst, but after that it was smooth sailing.

The following morning, we were in Nassau, the Bahamian national capital. It was a beautiful island paradise. I loved experiencing a whole new culture. We looked for treasures in the marketplace and bartered with the locals. Back on the ship, we hung out by the pool and had dinner at another one of the ship's restaurants, Animator's Palate. The coolest part was that, at first, the restaurant was all black and white, and the servers wore black pants and white vests; but by the end of the meal, the room had transformed to complete color—even the servers' vests had changed.

Every day brought more surprises and more fun. On our last day, we stopped at Disney's very own island called Castaway Cay. This meant that the only people on the island were other Disney cruisers, so we all had the island to ourselves. I loved the swaying palm trees, white sandy beaches, and crystal-clear blue waters.

Our family headed to the snorkeling lagoon, where we got our snorkeling gear, figured out how to put it on, and took a hilarious family picture. Most of the family didn't last long in the saltwater, and soon it was just Denise and me exploring the lagoon. I loved being in the water, a place where nobody stared at me and I felt free. If I could have bottled that moment in time, I would have.

We took pictures with the Disney characters and enjoyed the magical island atmosphere. I wished the day would never end, but before long it was time to pack up and head back to the ship for our last night on board.

OUR TRIP WAS nearly over, but we had one more special event planned. My brother Andy and his wife Michele were also vacationing in Florida, and they intended to meet up with us for a day at Sea World.

At Sea World, there was a lagoon where the dolphins swam near enough to splash the crowd. You could even touch a dolphin if you were close enough. I touched a few dolphins and got splashed a lot. We also saw dolphins, sea lions, and otters performing in shows. We especially loved the killer whale, Shamu, and saw two Shamu performances, one during the day and one at night.

Andy, Michele, Denise, and I even got to ride Kraken, a huge roller coaster where you sit with your feet dangling in the air. It was so much fun that we went twice.

The next day, Denise and her family returned home, but the rest of us had one more day left. I wanted to make the most of it. At the hotel pool, we swam and relaxed under the beautiful blue sky and big yellow sun. I tried not to think about the fact that I had another surgery scheduled when we returned to Minnesota, this time on my right lung. For now, I was just happy to be with my family and thankful that Make-A-Wish really had made my wishes come true.

UNIVERSITY OF MINNESOTA
CHILDREN'S HOSPITAL, FAIRVIEW

Fortunately, the lung surgery on my right lung went just as well as the previous ones had. Afterward, it was decided that instead of doing chemo we'd wait a month and check my scans. I planned on spending the next month doing as many fun things as I could. Whatever came my way, I knew I was going to be up for it. Nothing was ever planned; it was all spur-of-the-moment fun because I knew that in a month things could change yet again.

After having surgery, one thing you have to watch out for is the incision site. You need to make sure it's closing properly and not getting infected. Well, that was one thing I wasn't watching closely enough. In late June, I noticed the incision had all the signs of infection: redness, heat, swelling, and pain. When my mom called the hospital, they said I should be brought in immediately. My dad drove me back to Fairview, where the doctors started me on antibiotics and fluids to try to get the infection under control.

To make matters worse, I was supposed to go on a boat cruise on Lake Minnetonka as part of the "KS95 for Kids Radiothon" reunion. KS95 was a local radio station that held a radiothon each year to raise money for children's cancer research. I was so disappointed when I couldn't go.

Over the next two days, I was seen by a couple of doctors who tried to figure out what they should do about my incision. It wasn't getting better and seemed to be draining a little more. They stuffed dressings into the incision to absorb as much of the drainage as possible. Still, the incision didn't heal. I was worried because of the fungal infection I'd had on Shorty, and I knew I didn't want to go through anything like that again. At the same time, I felt that I was in the best hands, so I decided to leave it up to the doctors to worry about the infection for me.

Finally, on day five of my stay, the doctors switched to a calcium alginate wound dressing called AlgiSite. AlgiSite, a compound obtained from marine algae, was highly absorbent and biodegradable. This was something new to me, and I hoped it would work.

During what turned out to be another long hospital stay, I went to the annual Turtle Derby event at Fairview. This event was a really big deal for all the kids. Every year, the patients looked forward to picking out a turtle to cheer for and watching it race against everyone else's. The race was held in a little park area outside the hospital.

Before the race, a nurse unhooked me from my lines and I went to watch. I was so glad I could go. At the start of the derby, there were many competitions occurring at the same time, but toward the end, it all came down to the final round. To my surprise, my aunt Maureen and my great aunt Marcella arrived for a visit. I was glad we were able to have that time together. We shared laughs and good food—and there's nothing like the entertainment of a turtle! The derby lasted about three hours, and I stayed the whole time (anything to stay out of the hospital and away from being hooked up).

By day seven, my incision had started to look better. The seaweed was doing its job, and I was glad the doctors had decided to try it. I always said, "If you don't try something, you won't know if it's going to work or not." That's how I looked at chemo treatments or any other treatment, for that matter. I never wanted to have to sit and wonder if trying something would have worked after all. My motto had become "No Regrets and Never Give Up."

By this time, though, I was sick of being in the hospital. I started to feel emotionally down, and all I did was lie around. Who came to the rescue? Jill, one of my favorite nurses at Fairview. She brought her wiener dog, Coca, in for a visit. She knew Coca could cheer me up, and she was right. After that, I knew the coming days would be better.

As day ten approached, my counts were up and my incision looked good. I was out of there! My dad came to pick me up, as usual.

I actually had mixed emotions about going home. My incision was still open, and I worried that it could get worse. The doctors and nurses assured me that the homecare nurse would keep a close eye on the incision, and that put me a bit more at ease. I was told that my mom and I would be in charge of the dressing changes and that I would have to be on IV antibiotics three times a day. But none of that was new to me. By then, I could do my IVs in my sleep.

A week after my release from the hospital, I had to go back to see Dr. Neglia, also known as Uncle Joe. A group of doctors had consulted on my case and had come up with a plan. They thought the lung tumors that had been removed during my previous surgery weren't new; perhaps the tumors had been there all along but had only recently shown up on the scans. Based on this, the doctors wanted to wait another month to see if any new tumors appeared. I decided once again that the doctors knew best. And besides, it meant that for another month I could go back to being a normal kid.

AS THE NEXT checkup approached, I felt nervous but was confident that everything would be okay. Dr. Neglia looked at my chest scan and saw something unusual. He thought that it might be scar tissue, which worried me, but scar tissue was better than cancer. I hoped that the cancer had stayed away, that maybe it would stay away forever.

Dr. Neglia said, "I'll see you in another month." For now, I could go back to being my normal self again. That meant another month of having fun, and that was exactly what I intended to do.

ALBANY, MINNESOTA

I returned to school and did what any other sixteen-year-old did: hung out with friends, went to movies, and looked forward to becoming a licensed driver. Being sixteen meant this would be a big year for me. I intended to take a driver's education course, get my learner's permit, and then go for my driver's test.

At first, many people thought it would be impossible for me to drive because I didn't have a right leg. Was I going to let *that* stand in my way? Of course not. Nothing was going to hold me back from driving. I saw it as my destiny to be on the open road.

I had prosthetic leg, and some people thought I would need to have the car's floor pedals moved to accommodate this. Well, I was determined to learn to drive without having the floor pedals moved. I would learn to drive with my left leg instead.

I took driver's education classes along with my classmates. The class was only one week long, and I thought it was easy. I couldn't wait to finish it and take the exam. That day finally came, and I walked into the building with confidence. But I got nervous once I had the exam in hand. Those thirty-five questions on the piece of paper in front of me could make or break my driving career.

I flew through the questions and was done in just twenty-five minutes. Then I sat there and thought, *Did I do this wrong?* I thought maybe I had finished too fast, and the test seemed too easy. I turned in my test and got my results on the spot.

When the exam was handed back to me, I saw that I had passed. I was free to drive—with a licensed driver, of course. I now had my learner's permit, but it would be a few more months before I could get my actual driver's license. During the next six months, I practiced driving whenever I had the opportunity.

THE DAY OF MY driver's test finally arrived. I knew I could pass. I even drove to the licensing center in Paynesville. I told myself that nothing could stand in my way—not a driver's test, not anything. I was fighting for something much more important than this test. I was fighting for my life.

As I waited in the car for the examiner, I kept my cool. She started by making sure my turn signal lights worked—that was easy enough. Then she got in the car, and off we went. It was a smooth ride up until the parallel parking. As I was backing up, I bumped the traffic cone slightly. I wasn't sure the examiner had even noticed. So I continued parking, and in no time at all, it was over.

The examiner told me I'd passed. All that was left was getting my picture taken. I was now a licensed driver in the state of Minnesota.

UNIVERSITY OF MINNESOTA MEDICAL CENTER, RIVERSIDE CAMPUS

Just two days after the September 11 attacks on the World Trade Center, I made another trip to the hospital. I had a chest CT in the morning and an appointment with Dr. Neglia later on. He had bad news. The cancer was back.

He told me he was sorry that he always had to give me bad news, but he said he would find something that would work against the cancer. I had to be strong. My surgery, another thoracotomy, would take place in four days.

Because of the 9/11 disasters, the operating rooms at the University campus of the medical center were full. People from New York had been sent to Minnesota for surgery. This meant I had to go across the Mississippi River to the Riverside campus of the University of Minnesota Medical Center, where Dr. Leonard would operate on me. I had never been to that part of the medical center, and I didn't want to go. Nothing would be familiar there, and I wouldn't have the nurses on 5B to help me recover.

I decided to take a stand. I asked Dr. Leonard if I could have my surgery at the Riverside campus but be brought back to the University and 5B for my recovery. He agreed. That meant I would only have to be at Riverside for one night.

EARLY IN THE MORNING on September 17, I was back in the Twin Cities for surgery. My mom and dad accompanied me to Riverside. It was a quiet ride down.

We arrived at the Riverside campus on time and waited in the pre-op room. Everything was as it always was during prep and surgery, except that afterward I was sent to the pediatric ICU. The only thing I remembered about that day was waking up and asking Uncle Joe (Dr. Neglia) for a hug. Later, my mom told me that I asked him for a hug three times in a row, and each time he gave me one.

My sister Denise and her family came for a short visit to see how the surgery went. I don't remember much about their visit, but I knew they were there and that I would be okay because I had my nephew Brandon's hand to hold.

I also had my Beanie Baby named Hope. My sister's family had given me Hope, a small bear kneeling in prayer, long ago; during every surgery and hospital stay, I kept Hope with me for comfort and protection. Hope even had his own patient ID bracelet in case he ever got lost. Whenever I held Hope, I knew my family was with me.

That night, my family left so I could get some sleep. It was a rough night. I had a roommate, and all night long she cried and called out for people. I told myself to get through the night because in the morning I'd return to 5B. I watched the clock, which seemed to move more slowly than usual. I barely slept, I was in pain, and I just wanted the morning to come so I could leave.

AT QUARTER TO SIX the next morning, Dr. Leonard checked on me. I had held up my end of the bargain, and now it was his turn. I asked him if I could go back to 5B. He said no.

Dr. Leonard didn't want me to leave Riverside until my chest tube had come out, which wouldn't be for another two days. He only stayed a minute or so, and then he was gone. I started crying, which instantly increased my pain. Breathing wasn't easy with my chest tube, and now I was crying and needed extra air.

I really didn't want to be there, and I was determined to get out. Usually, I was a cooperative patient, but this time I wasn't going down without a fight. Shortly after Dr. Leonard left, I called my brother Andy. I told him the whole story and asked for his help. He told me he would do what he could.

Andy phoned Dr. Neglia, who was on call that morning, and told him the story. Dr. Neglia said that the University was prepared for my arrival and he didn't know what the hold-up was. I cried all morning and wouldn't give in. Finally, Dr. Neglia talked Dr. Leonard into letting me go over to 5B.

Not until mid-afternoon had everything been arranged. Dr. Leonard came by to tell me that I could go back to 5B. I already knew, but I said, "Thank you so much." I told him how much it meant for me to be on 5B, my second home.

The paramedics came to get me because I was going back to the University by ambulance. As I was leaving, I apologized repeatedly to my nurse at Riverside. I told her I was sorry for being such a pain. I just wanted to be with my familiar nurses and doctors (and besides, a deal is a deal).

On 5B, my nurse Melissa was there to greet me. I spent the next five days there; after that, I was on the mend and looked forward to going home.

Let your voice be heard.

Stand up for what you want and voice your opinion. Tell the doctors and nurses what you need for your recovery. You know yourself better than anyone. You're the judge of how you feel. Don't be afraid to stand tall and say what needs to be said.

COBORN CANCER CENTER, ST. CLOUD

Chemo alone wasn't doing the trick. It was time to try something new. Dr. Neglia suggested we give radiation a try, and I decided that what he said goes.

As a result of taking a new treatment direction, more doctors were going to be involved in my care. In November 2001, I was seen by Dr. Dusenbery from the Department of Therapeutic Radiology-Radiation Oncology at the University of Minnesota Medical School. My dad and I sat calmly in the waiting room. By this time, we were used to hearing all sorts of news, so we figured this wouldn't be so bad.

As soon as I met Dr. Dusenbury, I could tell how nice she was. She took notes about my case and looked at my scans. She thought radiation could help me. She had even better news—her medical school teacher was a radiation oncologist in St. Cloud, only twenty minutes away from where I lived. Dr. Dusenbury said I could get my radiation done at the Coborn Cancer Center in St. Cloud. This was great news because I wouldn't have to drive to the Twin Cities every day for a ten-minute radiation treatment. I was in the middle of my sophomore year of high school. I liked the idea of being treated closer to home so I could avoid long drives to Minneapolis and continue going to school.

I also started a nebulizer chemotherapy treatment, which meant I inhaled GM-CSF through a special machine called a nebulizer, two times a day for seven days, followed by seven days off. This form of chemo was part of a clinical trial at the Mayo Clinic in Rochester. In the clinical study, the doctors at Mayo hoped to learn about the effects of inhaled GM-CSF and its ability to stimulate the immune system to destroy osteosarcoma lung tumors. I wasn't part of the trial, but my doctors wanted me to try this form of chemo in addition to the radiation.

THE DAY ARRIVED when I was supposed to meet Dr. Meyers at Coborn. I was a little nervous about radiation, but I had been through so much already that I thought this could be easy in comparison.

When Dr. Meyers walked into the room, I liked him instantly. He knew how to talk to me and explain how the sessions would go. I learned that I would need thirty to thirty-five treatments of radiation on a spot in my left lung. Dr. Meyers explained some of the side effects of radiation (mainly being tired and having some small burns on my skin where the radiation went in), but they didn't sound too bad to me.

Before I could begin treatment, Dr. Meyers had to map out where he wanted the radiation to be directed. I had to have a few scans to help him find the path to the tumor; the goal was to hit the tumor but miss my heart and spine.

The mapping itself took a few visits. I had to lie on a cold table while Dr. Meyers drew lines on me, so that when I received the radiation I could be lined up perfectly in the same position every time. I thought to myself, *Please make good marks, and please find a good path that doesn't hit my heart and spine.* I asked God to guide the doctor's hands and mind. My prayer was answered because Dr. Meyers figured out a good angle for the radiation. I had faith in him and trusted him; I knew he would do a good job and figure out what would be best for me.

Once he had the right angle, I had to get three dots on my chest and one on each side of me. The doctor didn't use a marker because that would have washed off in the shower. Instead, I got tattoos to permanently mark where the radiation should go in. I hated that part because the tattoos hurt. I did my best to be brave.

I had to go back two more times so Dr. Meyers could check and double-check the mapping region he had created. Finally, I was ready to get my first radiation treatment.

I LAY ON THE TABLE while the radiologist positioned the machine and lined me up according to the tattooed marks. When asked if I was ready, I said, "Shoot."

Thoughts wandered through my mind. Dr. Meyers had said the radiation wouldn't hurt and that I would never know it was going into my body—but I wondered, *Would it hurt a little?* It didn't, though. In fact, I didn't feel anything and I couldn't see the radiation. I wondered how something so quick and simple could help me. I had been on hard doses of chemo that had made me sicker than I ever thought possible, and radiation seemed easy in comparison. I said to myself over and over, *Please work, please work, please work.* I just had to have faith.

In a quick ten minutes I was done. After that, I went to treatment five days a week. It was the same every time: line the dots up, shoot, and I was done.

Later on, when I completed radiation, I received a diploma saying I had graduated from radiation therapy. I thought that was pretty cool.

Keep hoping.

When one door closes, another will open. Make sure to go through it. You never know what's on the other side unless you have faith and take a chance.

ASPEN, COLORADO

The summer of 2002 brought an amazing opportunity. I was chosen to go to a camp in Aspen with other kids from Fairview. The camp was called the Silver Lining Ranch, and it specialized in giving kids with cancer a wonderful escape and a chance to have some fun in the great outdoors.

I had never been that far away from home without my family, and the idea made me kind of nervous, but I wanted to go. I needed my doctor's permission, and he said it was fine because I was in between chemo treatments and my counts and energy levels were high.

The night before my trip, I was packed and ready to go. I don't think I slept at all. I was high on energy and felt I could have run a marathon. The next morning, I was the first one up. I told my dad we had to hurry and get going or we would be late, even though we were way ahead of schedule. My dad loaded my bags in the car, I got a big hug from my mom, and we were off to the Twin Cities again—but this time for fun (since we were headed to the airport). I couldn't wait for my adventure to begin.

As we walked into the airport, I saw the group I was going with. There were seven of us altogether, including Nancy, my nurse practitioner. Soon it was time to fly. I said good-bye to my dad, and we boarded the plane.

We flew into Denver first, where we were met by the kids joining us from Chicago and Cincinnati. I made friends with two of them, Carolyn and Margo, right away. We played cards while waiting for the flight to Aspen. Once we arrived in Aspen, we boarded a bus and were off to the ranch.

I couldn't believe my eyes when we got there. The ranch house was huge, like a hotel. The welcoming room had homey decorations and an incredible view. Andrea Jaeger, the tennis player, was the cofounder and executive director of the camp. She gave us an orientation, and afterward we went to find our rooms. I was happy to discover that Carolyn and Margo would be my roommates—it was as if the staff knew before we did that we would click right away. Our room was awesome. The wall even had a monkey party mural on it.

Soon, I had almost forgotten I had cancer, which was the whole point of the camp. Chef John—the best chef ever— served spaghetti and garlic bread for dinner, and everyone got to know each other better. My roommates and I stayed up later than we were supposed to that night, talking about anything and everything.

OUR FIRST DAY'S ACTIVITIES included the ropes course with rock climbing, races with funny clothes, sumo wrestling, and more. I couldn't believe it when I took on the challenge of rock climbing. I was nervous, but as I hopped from rock to rock my fear disappeared. I had only made it halfway up the wall when my breathing became heavy and my lips started to turn blue. The high altitude and thin air got to me, so the counselors told me to come down and rest.

Next, we went on a gondola ride up and down the mountain;

it was the most amazing experience. I was glad I was able to share the moment with Carolyn and Margo, and also Patrick and Jen, two of the camp counselors. The view was breathtaking as we drifted over Aspen and ascended the mountain. At the top, we took pictures and had a picnic lunch. Time seemed to fly by and, before I knew it, we were heading down the mountain.

Back at the ranch, we had a tournament in the game room. We bowled and played Ping-Pong, basketball, air hockey, pool, and more. In basketball, I took second place. But it wasn't about the winning—it was all about the fun. That night, we headed to the famous Boogie's Diner for dinner and milkshakes. All the girls sat in one booth, and all the guys piled around the tables. As the day wound down, it was back to the ranch and off to bed, where my two new friends and I talked the night away.

The next day, we went horseback riding. I had never ridden a horse before, and I was excited to try something new. One of the assistants helped me onto Ranger, my horse. He was a gentle horse who took good care of me as we went up and down Snowmass Mountain. We all rode in single file, like kindergarten kids walking down the hall.

The afternoon included a pool party, with volleyball and basketball games. I couldn't stop thinking about how much fun I was having; it was like I was a normal person doing normal, fun things again. That night, we made tiles to hang on the wall, each with our own design. Mine was simple, with only my name on it.

I WAS THE FIRST ONE up in the morning because we were going whitewater rafting, and I couldn't wait. I had never been whitewater rafting, but it involved water and I loved water, so

I was all for it. After making an equipment stop for life vests and helmets, we headed for the rapids. Everyone looked cute dressed up, like one big, happy family.

When we arrived, the boats were already lined up and we were put in our groups. My group included Margo, Carolyn, Jen, and Patrick, and our boat was the first to load. After we were all situated, we headed out over the warm, refreshing waters, and I felt as if my life couldn't have gotten any better.

It wasn't long before we rammed into rapids. I almost fell in the water two times, but because I was all for falling in, I didn't mind a bit. Soon, we were a little ahead of the other groups so we pulled over to the side and waited for the others to catch up. We had so much fun in our boat, laughing and talking along the way. As we neared the end of our ride, I was sad it was nearly over. We returned to the ranch, where everyone took it easy for the rest of the day.

Another day of adventure awaited us. The next morning, Andrea taught us to play tennis. We volleyed the ball back and forth and played for prizes. We also went to the actor Kevin Costner's home to fish, but he wasn't there. I loved fishing, but I was never into touching the fish. It worked out fine that day, though, because I didn't catch a thing. Later, we went out for a night on the town.

On our last day at camp, I wanted it all to go as slowly as possible so the trip wouldn't have to end. My friends and I got up to see the sunrise. We talked about our feelings and what it was like living with cancer. It felt good knowing that others felt the same way I did: that cancer was a battle we could fight and win.

That day, we shopped in Aspen, the perfect mountain setting. The girls took off in one direction, and the guys all went in the other. Later, we met at the bus and cruised back to the ranch for some free time. I didn't want to pack and leave, and neither did anyone else. We had all became great friends and had fun together, sharing unforgettable moments.

We had a talent show that night, with skits, songs, and dancing. It was a great way to end a perfect trip. We also watched our own movie—a videotape of our adventures from the beginning of camp to the end. We were told that we would all receive a copy of the tape after we returned home. When we were tucked in for the last night of camp, my roomies and I stayed up late into the night talking once again. We were going to miss each other.

THE MOOD WAS SOMBER the morning we left. Everyone said their good-byes at the airport, with lots of hugs. I was happy to be heading back to my family, yet I wanted to be at the ranch. I'd had the time of my life there.

Still, it was back to the fight and I was ready. I would go at it with 110 percent. Nothing was going to stop me now.

UNIVERSITY OF MINNESOTA
CHILDREN'S HOSPITAL, FAIRVIEW

After I had completed my radiation treatment, things calmed down for the next ten months. My routine included chemo, transfusions of platelets and blood, infections, and lots of high and low points. There was nothing new except for one thing: I was now on chemo that I carried around in a bag. That allowed me to be at home and not in the hospital during treatments.

In October 2003, I went to Fairview for scans and a regular checkup and, this time, the results weren't good. My lung tumor was on the move again and growing.

Dr. Neglia said that he wanted to have the tumor removed—it had become too large to treat. Surgery was my best option. By this time, hearing that I needed surgery was no big deal. I'd already had a bunch of thoracotomies—what was one more? However, Dr. Neglia had another doctor lined up to do this surgery: Dr. Maddaus, Professor of Surgery in the Division of Cardiovascular and Thoracic Surgery at the University of Minnesota. Dr. Maddaus was the only doctor in the world able to do certain surgeries. I learned that the operation I now faced was much more complicated and difficult than any I'd had so far.

I needed the surgery, but it quickly became a waiting game because Dr. Maddaus was always booked solid or out of town. This was frustrating at times, but I worked through it by relying heavily on my family. Just being around them and hearing their encouraging words helped me keep going and calmed my nerves.

On October 22, my dad and I headed to the hospital for more scans. That was the day I met with Dr. Maddaus for the first time. He was very straightforward and professional, but he was obviously used to dealing with adult patients. I knew he meant business by the look on his face when he told me the surgery wouldn't be easy. My mind flooded with emotion; I held it in and tried to be strong. My brother was there with us, and so was Nancy, my nurse practitioner.

Dr. Maddaus said that the surgery would take place in November. Three specialized doctors were to be involved. Dr. Maddaus would be the main surgeon, another doctor would do the part of the surgery involving the veins, and lastly, Dr. Ogilvie, from the Division of Cardiovascular and Thoracic Surgery, was needed because the tumor had worked its way around major vessels and veins and was pressed against my spinal cord. Dr. Maddaus explained all of the details, and by the time he had finished, I thought I might pass out. He said I would lose lots of blood, but they would transfuse me when needed. There was a chance that the bleeding wouldn't stop and I'd never make it out of the OR.

The door of the room we sat in was cracked open slightly. Dr. Neglia passed by, and then stopped in to see how things were going. He must have known from our expressions that Dr. Maddaus had told us everything. Dr. Neglia said he would return in a little while. My dad and brother sat there, not knowing what to say. They were scared, but they tried not to show it.

This was going to be the biggest, scariest, most critical surgery I'd ever had. I knew this surgery would take all the strength I had stored up and absolutely everything I had left to give. Dr. Maddaus told me the surgery would be more painful than any of my previous surgeries.

After Dr. Maddaus left, I broke down crying. The news was a lot to handle at my age. In an instant, my life was no longer about normal teenage things but about survival. The strength I would need to get through this was something I would have to dig deep for.

Dr. Neglia came back to check on us and said everything was going to be fine. He told us that Dr. Maddaus was a great surgeon and would take excellent care of me in the OR. Dr. Neglia said Dr. Maddaus would do everything in his power to make sure the surgery went well. I asked Dr. Neglia if he could come into the OR once or twice to check on me during my surgery. He said it would be no problem, which made me feel better. I pulled myself together and was able to leave the clinic.

On the car ride home, my dad and I were quiet; we had a lot of information to take in. I had to tell my mom the news once we got home. I knew she'd take it hard, but she seemed to do okay. She was hurting on the inside and would probably get little sleep that night. My mom and I didn't talk about the surgery much. I felt that I would be better off dealing with my fears on my own.

It was a rough night for me, but I began to think the surgery might just be my ticket to beating my cancer. Maybe if the tumor was removed, there wouldn't be any other tumors afterward, and maybe the nightmare would be over. I knew it was a slim chance, but it was a chance, and that was enough for me.

BEFORE SURGERY, I had to have a bunch of different scans—a bone scan, a chest CT, a pulmonary function test, X-rays, and more. Dr. Maddaus wanted to know exactly what he was dealing with before he went in. The more he knew, the better the surgery would go.

As the day got closer, my emotions became harder and harder to deal with. Most of the time, I was fine but when I started thinking about all the things that could go wrong, I'd just flip out. I had tons of anxiety and my stress level was beyond even my limit. I had always tried to be a positive person, but it was really hard with so many scary thoughts rolling around in my head.

During the days leading up to the surgery, I tried to forget about what was going to happen. I still needed to function and deal with everyday life, including going to school. It was hard to concentrate on math problems when I was thinking about the biggest surgery of my life. I toughened up and tried to ignore my fears. That was the only way I could get through it all.

NOVEMBER 13 ARRIVED, and there was no turning back. I worked up all the strength I had and felt all the prayers being sent my way. I knew that if fate were ever going to have a hand in things, this was going to be the day.

Early that morning, I met with Dr. Ogilvie, who explained how the surgery would go. He said it would start with Dr. Maddaus and the vascular surgeon making an incision on my front side to open my chest and separate all the veins, muscles, and nerves. All of this would take about five to six hours. At that point, they would call in Dr. Ogilvie to separate the tumor from one of my ribs in the front. After that, they would close me up, flip me over, and make another incision on my back so Dr. Ogilvie could continue to separate the tumor from my bones. He said he would need to shave five or more of my vertebra to have clear margins. The hope was that there were no veins in this tumor supplying my spine with blood, because if the doctors had to cut through that, then I could become very weak or, worse yet, paralyzed. Once all of this was done, the doctors would lift the tumor out and close me up, around midnight. I would spend the night in the pediatric ICU.

Dr. Ogilvie said he had complete confidence in Dr. Maddaus and that they wouldn't attempt this surgery unless they thought it would be successful. After hearing what he had to say, I felt better. I had made peace with the fact that it would take all of this to get the tumor out, and I decided I would do whatever needed to be done.

My friends Savannah and Catherine had come with my family to be with me until I was taken into the OR. They were such great friends and had supported me every step of the way. I was glad that Catherine and Savannah were there; otherwise, I think I would have worried about the situation too much. When I started to feel sick during pre-op, Catherine, Savannah, and my family managed to get me laughing. I even had a surprise visitor, Josie, one of the nurses from 5B. She stopped in to wish me good luck before starting her shift. Seeing her helped me feel better.

Two hours later, the moment arrived. I started to get sick, but I was given medication to calm my nerves. I got hugs from everyone, not knowing if I would ever see them again.

As I was wheeled down to the OR, I made eye contact with the nurse who would be with me during the operation. I felt empty inside. I truly didn't know if I would be alive at the end of the day, but I knew I was going to fight my hardest through this surgery. A single tear rolled down my cheek and I was out, at the mercy of the surgeons.

Say a prayer, or ask others to say prayers for you.

There were many times when I prayed to God to help me
or to be with me when I went through surgery. I prayed for
Him to watch over me and all of my friends who had cancer
or other illnesses. When I went into surgery, I asked Him
to help the surgeons make the right decisions and not to let
me die. I told Him I wanted to do so much more with my
life—go to college, get married, have a family, and be a nurse.
I asked Him for help, and I thanked Him whenever I got a
miracle or had a prayer answered. I have never blamed God
that I have cancer. Yes, the doctors helped to keep me alive,
and I kept myself alive by fighting, but God has had a hand
in it, too. Only He truly knew everything about where my
journey would take me.

PEDIATRIC ICU, UNIVERSITY OF MINNESOTA CHILDREN'S HOSPITAL, FAIRVIEW

I was alive. I was *alive*. I had made it through. I woke up and felt the breathing tube in my throat. It was painful; I wanted it out. I started shaking my head. I heard the nurses tell me I was okay. I still wanted the tube out. I heard a doctor in the background telling the nurse to keep a close eye on me in case I tried to pull out the tube myself.

I COULDN'T OPEN my eyes; there was a lubricant on them used to keep them from drying out during surgery. I heard the calming sound of my mom and sister next to me. I couldn't talk to them yet because of the tube, so I developed my own way of communicating. My sister would go through the alphabet, and I'd nod my head at the right letter.

I WAS STILL UNDER the effects of too much muscle relaxant, which disabled my movements. When the doctor came in and asked me to touch his hand, which was right above mine, I couldn't move my arm. I could move my fingers, though, and I knew that was a good sign.

I still wasn't breathing on my own. The machine the breathing tube was hooked up to did the breathing for me. The doctor was concerned that if he took the tube out too early, I wouldn't be able to control my breathing. He gave it some more time, and when the doctor came back in again later, I was ready. I touched his hand and blew air through the tube. He said the tube could come out, and when it did, I took a deep breath of warm, invigorating air. The doctor stayed a few more minutes, watching to make sure I continued to breathe on my own.

The rest of the night was a blur. All I knew was that I had done it. I'd survived the surgery, my tube was out, and once again I was on the road to recovery.

THE NEXT MORNING, I woke up feeling like a truck was parked on my chest. The nurse gave me an extra dose of morphine to keep me comfortable. The next time I woke up, my mom was sitting next to me. She said, "You have a visitor." It was Dr. Neglia. I was so happy to see him.

He said the surgery was successful and had been completed several hours earlier than expected. As it turned out, the tumor was located in a better position than they'd originally thought, so Dr. Ogilvie had never even come into the operating room. The doctors had completed the operation without having to turn me over or make an incision in my back. The tumor had slid right out. The doctors were pleased with the surgery, and I was so excited about the news that I felt like jumping up and hugging Dr. Neglia.

The doctors expected me to be in the ICU for several days, and in the hospital for a few weeks. I think they forgot who they were dealing with. I planned to get out of there as soon as I could. Within twenty-four hours, I was in good enough shape to leave the ICU and go back to 5B.

My parents knew I was in good hands, so they left. Aunt Maureen arrived and ended up spending the night with me on 5B. It gave me comfort having her there, not only because she was my aunt but also because she was a nurse. Who better to have stay with me?

5B, PEDIATRIC ONCOLOGY FLOOR, UNIVERSITY OF MINNESOTA CHILDREN'S HOSPITAL

Just two days after surgery, I had started moving around and was sitting up for short periods of time. The doctors and nurses were very impressed with my recovery. I was a week ahead of schedule.

The surgeons wanted a scan of my chest. When my nurse Amy told me this, I started to cry because I knew how much it would hurt to have the X-ray technicians move me around. Amy said she'd come with me, and my brother Andy was there, too. Amy and Andy helped me through the whole procedure, because I was very weak. Afterward, I got back into bed and slept for the rest of the day.

DURING MY TIME in the hospital, the Dawn of a Dream gala took place. This fundraising event sponsored by the Children's Cancer Research Fund (CCRF) included an award ceremony, which I was supposed to attend. I had won their annual butterfly contest based on a butterfly I had drawn. The butterfly was a symbol of hope and transformation. I never even dreamed I would win when I drew it—I was just drawing from my heart, and whatever came out came out.

Before my surgery, a camera crew had come to make a tape of me so the video could be a part of the Dawn of a Dream program. When the night of Dawn of a Dream arrived, my mom was at the hospital to stay with me. My dad, my sister Denise, my brother Andy, and his wife Michele would all attend the event on my behalf. My dad looked sharp in his suit and bowtie, while my sister was all decked out in a beautiful long sparkly gown. Andy and Michele looked amazing in their formal wear as well.

Before the event, Van Patrick, a DJ from the local KS95 radio station stopped by with his wife Lori. Van always spent time helping to raise money for children's cancer research and had hosted the "KS95 for Kids Radiothon." I thought it was great that Van and Lori came to see me.

Later, as I was watching television, I got a phone call; it was my brother holding up his cell phone during the gala so I could hear what was going on. A song was being dedicated to me, and my videotape was playing in the background. I heard it all, so, in a way, I did get to be there that night. I'm glad my dad, my sister, my brother, and my sister-in-law were able to go in my place; it made me feel good to know they were there representing me. And I was really happy that my family could be a part of such a special night.

AFTER ONLY SIX DAYS of recovery, I was discharged from the hospital. That had to be a record. I was happy to be going home. It was still painful for me to move, but I knew I could handle it. I wanted to be able to see my friends and get back to school.

The fight was constant, but I was determined not to let the cancer win.

ALBANY, MINNESOTA

In December 2003, I was in the hospital with the flu. I had hardcore headaches, threw up, slept all day, and coughed. I had to be treated with antibiotics and other medications. But around that time, a different symptom showed up. My left arm hurt between the wrist and elbow. When I mentioned this to the doctor on call, he looked at my arm but thought I had probably slept on it wrong. So I stopped thinking about it.

Later that month, I went back to the Coborn Cancer Center in St. Cloud for radiation treatments on my left lung. At this point, getting radiation was no big deal for me. It was what I had to do to stay alive.

My left arm still bothered me, though. In January, I started taking medication for the pain. I knew something wasn't right. I could feel a bump there, or at least what I thought was a bump. I kept it to myself for a few more weeks and tried to live a normal life, going to school and being with friends.

DURING MY NEXT radiation visit, I was seen by a different doctor and I asked him to take a look at my left arm. I pointed out the area that hurt, and he felt around for tender spots. He could tell it involved the bone, and he thought it would be best if I got an X-ray.

The following day, after my radiation treatment, I got the X-ray at the clinic. I wasn't too concerned at this point. The nurse told me to call the following day for the scan results. I went home and kept quiet. I had only told my sister Denise about the pain in my arm and the scans. I didn't want my parents to have to worry.

DURING LUNCH PERIOD at school the next day, I called the nurse to find out if my scans had been read. She told me the scans had been faxed to Dr. Meyers, who had seen something in the cortex, or middle, of my bone. Dr. Meyers wanted me to get an MRI done as soon as possible.

I hung up the phone. I was frustrated. I thought, *Great, now what's wrong with me? If it isn't one thing, it's another.*

I didn't have much time to sit and think, though. I still had to get my blood drawn for the day, like I did every Monday and Thursday during my lunch period. I went to the Albany Hospital as usual, but because I had spent half of my lunch period on the phone already, I had to rush to get back to my next class on time.

After I returned, I had to sit through two more classes, knowing something wasn't right with my arm. I had a test that day, and it was hard to concentrate. I felt frustrated inside, but I tried not to show it on the outside. I preferred to handle my problems on my own and not worry other people. I got through my classes and went home. After finishing my homework that night, I told myself, *Tomorrow is another day.*

ON JANUARY 16, I had my usual radiation, but afterward I was supposed to have the MRI. That meant I would get home later than usual. I still didn't want to tell my mom where I was going, so I said I would be at Denise's.

It was a typical school day, and I didn't think about the MRI at all. I knew I needed to stay focused on school, so I locked the door on all the bad thoughts.

After school, I went to get the radiation and then headed to the St. Cloud Hospital. I checked in. I proceeded to the waiting area, where I was told that an ICU patient had just gone in before me, so my wait would be an extra hour. This meant I'd be there until late. I knew I had to call my parents and tell them the truth about where I was.

Turns out, my sister had already told our parents because she felt they needed to know. When I talked to my dad, he wasn't upset and only voiced his concern. I felt much better, knowing I didn't have to hide what was going on anymore. I went to the hospital cafeteria and then watched some TV. I was calm, taking things as they came.

When I was finally called in for the MRI, I got up onto the table and was strapped in so I couldn't move. At first, my mind was clear. I picked my choice of music to listen to during the scan. The radiologist put the headphones on me and pushed me into the tube.

As I lay there, I had flashbacks about my first MRI, back when my right leg had hurt and I found out I had cancer. Would it be just like that? Was something bad going to happen? I didn't want to think about it and tried to concentrate on the music. It was a long forty minutes on the table.

Dr. Meyers would read the scan that night. He had given me his cell phone number so I could call him. I drove home praying that the scan results would be okay. When I got home, I put on a happy face. No one knew how worried I truly was, and that's the way I wanted it.

LATER THAT NIGHT, I called Dr. Meyers. He had read the scans. He said there was something in my left arm that appeared to be the same as what had once been on my right rib. I wasn't quite sure what he meant but kept listening. He told me they would be able to treat it with radiation. At that point, I still didn't get what "it" was, but I didn't ask. Dr. Meyers said he had already spoken to Dr. Neglia, and they both agreed on the treatment I should have. Dr. Meyers said Dr. Neglia was keeping his pager on in case I wanted to talk to him.

After thanking Dr. Meyers, I immediately called Dr. Neglia. When he answered his page, the first question he asked was, "Are you okay?" I said, "What is it? What's in my arm?" In a calm tone, Dr. Neglia said, "It's cancer."

The cancer had spread to a whole new area; it was in my arm. My world had turned upside down again, and I started shaking. Dr. Neglia reassured me that radiation was the right plan. I didn't know what to say. I was in shock because I hadn't thought of the pain in my arm as cancer. How did it get to my arm? Dr. Neglia told me that osteosarcoma can spread to other bones in the body.

Again Dr. Neglia asked if I was okay. I told him I was. He said he'd keep his pager on all weekend if I needed to talk. He encouraged me and said we wouldn't give up—we had come too far already, and he would find something to help me. I was scheduled to see him the following week for a bone scan. I thanked him and said good-bye. I knew I was in good hands.

Then I cried my eyes out, not knowing where to turn. I had battled the cancer so long, and now it had moved to a different area. How would I go on? I told myself I wasn't giving up and wouldn't let the cancer win. The cancer had no idea how long and hard I'd fight to win.

I called Denise and told her the cancer had spread. She was devastated and said I didn't deserve this. She said I'd been fighting so long and hard that I shouldn't have to go through this any longer. I deserved a cure. Denise wanted me to tell our parents, but I wasn't ready.

For two days, I tried to hold it together. I cried a bunch of times. Denise and her family came over to help me break the news to our mom and dad. I couldn't say it, though. Denise had to tell them.

They reacted quietly and calmly to the news. My mom said she had known something was wrong; she said I'd been too quiet lately, and she could see it in my eyes that something wasn't right. My mom and dad hugged me and helped me calm down. Now I was back on the road to fighting the cancer.

Dr. Meyer's treatment plan included twelve sessions of radiation to my arm. I was ready for the challenge. I told myself I could get through these treatments and fight this battle, but it was the war I wanted to win.

Three days before I was due to begin the radiation treatments, I started coughing up blood. I almost fainted at the sight. Why in the world was I coughing up blood? I panicked. It was late at night, and I yelled for my parents. They came running. They were both worried and told me to take a deep breath. The blood was bright red, which meant something was bleeding inside me. I was scared that my lungs would fill up with blood, so I continued to cough up as much as I could. Soon I had coughed up about a cup of bright red blood.

We called Dr. Neglia, and he said not to panic but to come directly to Fairview. My dad and I headed out the door. By the time we were on the road, I had stopped coughing up blood and was calmer.

I tried to sleep on the way. I was exhausted. I needed to rest because I didn't know how much sleep I'd be able to get once I was at the hospital.

5B, PEDIATRIC ONCOLOGY FLOOR, UNIVERSITY OF MINNESOTA CHILDREN'S HOSPITAL

I went to the emergency room and checked in. Then it was straight to the pediatric ICU.

Dr. Neglia had made sure that everyone was ready for me. Right away, I was hooked up to machines that monitored my oxygen level, blood pressure, and pulse. The X-ray machine was on the way up as I arrived, and a chest X-ray was taken. My dad had to leave because parents weren't allowed to stay in the ICU at night. I was going to be monitored all night, but by now the blood had stopped coming up and things were looking better.

The following day, I was checked by a fleet of doctors; everyone needed to take a look. I was used that. When you're in the hospital, nothing stays a secret and your life becomes an open book. This didn't bother me because the more the doctors and nurses knew, the better the treatment they could give. I stayed in the pediatric ICU for half the day, and then transferred over to my second home, 5B.

On 5B my nurse Jody let me know that I needed to have an angiogram a week later. She had always been the one to tell me if my treatment would include something difficult, and I could take the news better with her by my side. She said the angiogram was a surgery where they'd stick a needle into a large vein by my groin area, and then feed a catheter up through my veins and into my lungs, where they'd inject a dye that would be visible in X-ray pictures. The dye would help the doctors determine where the blood I coughed up had come from. She said the blood could have been from a weak vessel or from a tumor falling apart.

Jody told me that after the angiogram I would have to lie flat for six hours to make sure the vein in my groin healed. I said, "Are you crazy? Lie still for six hours?" She laughed and said I'd be fine. I was able to leave the hospital the next morning and was back to my usual arm and lung radiation treatments that afternoon.

A WEEK LATER, I returned to Fairview for the angiogram. I had a question on my mind, *How would I go to the bathroom if I had to lie still for six hours?* I asked the nurse, and she said I'd be able to use a bedpan. I didn't like that idea at all. She told me I would get fluids in the OR, and I didn't know how my bladder was going to be able to hold it all. The nurse said I'd be fine, but I worried that I'd wake up from the procedure and have to go to the bathroom immediately.

Upon waking, I was in a lot of pain—not from the angiogram itself but because I had to pee so badly I thought I could explode. In a slurred, sleepy voice, I said, "I have to go to the bathroom," but no one heard me. I said it again, and still no one heard. I tried raising my voice, and finally someone got me a bedpan. Would you believe that after all that, I couldn't go? Sometimes anesthesia has that effect. I told myself I *had* to go, and after that I couldn't pee fast enough. Yet, when I was done, I still felt like I had to go.

I lay there until they took me up to 5B, where I was greeted by one of my favorite nurses, Carol, who would be my nurse for the day. As she prepared my room, hooked up my lines, and made me comfortable in bed, I realized I still had to go to the bathroom. She retrieved the bedpan and I went. Fifteen minutes later, I had to go again and we repeated this process several times for the next three hours.

Well, guess what? I found out later that during the angiogram they didn't even use the vein by my groin—they used the big one in my neck. So, as it turns out, I hadn't needed to lie still for six hours. What a ripoff! I chuckled over the whole thing, though. At least the surgery was over.

During this stay, I went to the cafeteria with Carol and learned a couple of tricks. First, you should always weigh your Rice Krispies bar before you buy it so you can get the biggest one. Second, fill up your soda, drink some, and then fill it up again before paying. Carol and I had a lot of laughs—we were two goofballs, made for each other.

I spent one night in the hospital after the angiogram. The next day, I was back on track with radiation to my arm and lung. Soon after, I was my old self again, goofing off, having fun, and living each day to the fullest.

Take life one day at a time.

Live in the moment. Happiness comes in small doses. Enjoy the opportunities you are given to have fun. Do what you can, when you can. And be thankful for the support team you have.

WALT DISNEY WORLD, ORLANDO, FLORIDA

Little did I know that after I finished radiation, I'd get to go to Florida again. Two moms I knew from the hospital, Merilee and Juli, created the Amy Mareck Fan Club. These two amazing moms had daughters with the same type of cancer I had, and they understood all I was facing. Merilee and Juli wanted to add a little cheer to my life, so they started taking up donations to put toward a trip to Disney World for my family and me. This meant I'd get to go on vacation one more time before I started my next big rounds of chemo. The trip was a gift I never saw coming.

In February 2004, my parents, my friend Savannah, and I were off to warm, sunny Florida. An unexpected perk on the airplane ride was that we sat next to some very cute boys. When we arrived in Florida late at night, we found out that Merilee and Juli had arranged for us to have a convertible rental car. A convertible! I was in heaven. However, our luggage didn't fit in it. The only vehicles available were minivans. A minivan? How does a person go from a convertible to a minivan? I started laughing and couldn't stop.

We stayed at Disney's Port Orleans Resort. I was once again in my "happy place," and cancer was the furthest thing from my mind.

Our days were filled with the sights and sounds of Disney. We hit all the major theme parks, including Epcot Center, the Magic Kingdom, Animal Kingdom, and Disney-MGM Studios. We went on rides like Test Track, Rock 'n' Roller Coaster, and Splash Mountain—and we did most of it in the rain. I didn't care about the weather, though. I was in Florida! Savannah and I even sat by the pool wearing long pants and sweatshirts. All around us, the Floridians had on heavy jackets, gloves, and winter hats. That just made us smile, thinking of our weather in Minnesota.

One rainy night, Savannah and I were returning to the resort in our rental van, and it was really dark. Florida law stated that you had to have your vehicle lights on when it was raining, and I thought ours *were* on. (I just assumed they were because my car at home had lights that went on automatically whenever the car was started.) Well, the headlights on the minivan *weren't* automatic, so we were driving around with no lights. I had thought it was awfully dark and hard to see, but I chalked it up to the weather. Two teenagers, driving in their minivan with no lights on—what a sight that would have been for the cops. (Uh, sorry officer, we didn't know!) When we returned to our room and told my parents the story, we all had a good laugh about it.

DURING THE TRIP, we went to dinner shows like the "Spirit of Aloha," a Polynesian luau set in the beachfront backyard at our resort. We saw Cirque Du Soleil, where amazing acrobats stunned the crowd. Savannah and I also made time for DisneyQuest, an indoor theme park filled with five floors of interactive games. You could even design your own roller coaster and take a virtual ride.

In just one week, we did all that and went to Universal Studios theme park and Sea World. Savannah and I went on every ride we could at Universal Studios, and I learned that it's not a good idea to go on the Incredible Hulk roller coaster followed right away by the Dueling Dragons roller coaster. (Let's just say, I made friends with the toilet afterward.) Sea World was incredible because I got to touch dolphins, my favorite creatures. Their skin felt like smooth rubber, and I could have spent hours watching them. I dreamed that someday I could swim with the dolphins.

Because I'd had chemo right before we left for vacation, I needed to have my blood drawn and get platelets three different times during the trip. Each time, my dad and I went to the Orlando Regional Healthcare Clinic, which was a whole new adventure. When we first drove up to the clinic, I wasn't sure if we were in the right spot because the building looked like a house. But it was the right place, and I thought it was kind of cool in a way. I had the same nurse each time, and she made sure everything was set up beforehand so I wouldn't have to stay long.

The vacation was just what I needed. The trip gave me the fuel to handle my next rounds of chemo. I would head into my treatments with a positive attitude and more determination than ever.

ALBANY, MINNESOTA

Try being a teenager working through school and doing all the typical teen things like going to football games, going to parties, and hanging out with friends; then try doing all that with cancer, chemo treatments, being sick, and having to grow up too fast. It was a challenge I was willing to face head on.

Keeping up with school while being sick and getting chemo was hard work. I spent many grueling hours trying to keep up with my classes. I would sometimes fall a week or two behind, but I never stopped trying to catch up. Occasionally, I even worked my way ahead of the class, but that didn't happen very often.

Some of my teachers went out of their way to help me. They got me what I needed, gave me extra tutoring when I didn't understand the material, and always kept me up to date on what was going on in class. Some teachers even came to my house to help me out.

However, I did have a couple of teachers who weren't so supportive and understanding, and that was really difficult. My parents got involved and let the school know that I was doing my best under the circumstances, working hard, and completing the assignments but that I couldn't do all of it myself. My mom was a lot of help when it came to teaching me geometry and algebra, but there was only so much we could do on our own. One teacher ignored the fact that I was obviously ill—I had no hair, always wore a cap, and had a chemo bag with a tube sticking out, but this teacher didn't seem to care. When my parents talked to him about my condition, he said it "wasn't his problem." There were many days when I wanted to give up, but I didn't. I knew I had to stick with it so I could graduate with my class on time.

I actually loved being in school because I was with my friends. Having cancer taught me a lot about finding my true friends. I was their friend because of what was on the inside, not because of how I looked on the outside. All of my friends were great, and each one supported me in a special way. They were there when I needed to talk or when I needed a good laugh.

Sometimes, though, I wondered if certain people were my friends because they *wanted* to be or because they felt sorry for me. It wasn't as if I expected everyone to like me, and I was sure there were some people who weren't fond of me—but I could accept that. Some people don't have it in them to love everyone in the world, but I certainly thought I'd try.

With my true friends, we were totally comfortable with each other and we could even joke about my having only one leg. Some of my guy friends even came up with nicknames for me, like flamingo. It was okay, though, because I had fun with it. I was the kind of person who accepted what I had and didn't dwell on the past or what could have been. It was the *future* I dreamed of.

Once, when our school held a pep rally, anyone who wore slippers got to tape a teacher to the wall for fun. When I went up there with a couple of my friends, one of my guy friends said, "Amy, you can't go up there, they said *slippers* and you have only one slipper." It was all in good fun.

There were times when my friends would ask me serious questions. I always tried to be straight with them and tell them what they wanted to know.

Whenever I was gone for any length of time, I knew my friends would be there for me when I got back. They kept me sane while I was going through everything—they were my support. People may come and go throughout life, but true friends are there forever.

SENIOR YEAR, I was back where I had once started, getting all the heavy-duty chemos again. But this time, my body handled it pretty well. I didn't have much nausea or throwing up; I was just tired a lot. I was afraid, but I walked past my fear with pride and with my head held high.

While going through heavy chemo, I was back to tutoring myself. I got my assignments and tried to figure them out; my mom helped when she could. I went to school when-ever possible. I hated missing any time during my senior year; it was supposed to be the best year—the year of ruling the school. On days when I had to stay home or was in the hospital, I tried not to think about all I was missing and focused instead on doing what I had to do to graduate.

Graduation was scheduled for the end of May. My doctor and I had it all planned out: I would get chemo right before graduation so that I'd have no side effects except fatigue when the big day came.

My counts didn't work with me, though—the entire month of May went by without any chemo. This was good and bad: good, because now I would be "healthy" and have a high energy level when I graduated, and bad because I didn't know what was happening on the inside of me. I was worried because it had been a whole month without any chemo, and my cancer could be spreading or growing. Elisa, one of my nurses, reassured me that the tumor probably wouldn't grow because my counts were down. I listened to her and tried to stop worrying.

MAY 28 WAS the day of the graduation ceremony for the Albany High School class of 2004. I was going to graduate on time.

That morning, we practiced so everyone would know where to go, what to do, and when to do it. The big night was only nine hours away. I was a little nervous—all I wanted to do was to make it up on the stage, walk across, and make it back down the stairs without falling.

Before the ceremony that night, we had a graduation party at my house. I invited some people from the Twin Cities, along with a few nurses, some neighbors, and family members. "Auntie Jill," one of my nurses from 5B, even brought her wiener dog, Coca. Everyone talked, shared stories, and gave me presents to open. After opening gifts, I looked at the clock and realized I was behind schedule and needed to get ready. I hurried to my room and put on my black pants and white shirt, along with my cap and gown. My dad drove me to the school and dropped me off so I could join the other graduating students before the ceremony.

When I thought about it, I was proud of what I had accomplished. I had done it, and this was going to be our night. My friends and I took a few pictures beforehand, but soon we were called to our places.

Now it was time to wait. We stood in line for forty-five minutes before we actually had to go on stage. Everyone was nervous and excited. All of a sudden, I heard, "Shh, it's time!"

As we started out, I thought about how this was the last time I'd walk down the hall as a student of Albany High School. I felt sad about it. I would never be in the pod area in front of the classrooms with all my friends again. It was all over with now, and everyone would move on and go their separate ways. I would start a new chapter of my life, and it would be a challenge. But I was always up for life's challenges.

Soon, it was my turn to walk in with my partner. I heard the graduation song playing in the background and saw the cameras flashing. I felt like we were walking down the red carpet. We were in the spotlight, and I walked slowly, making sure I knew where I was stepping so I wouldn't trip. I made it to my seat. Perfect, now I had only one task left—making it across the stage.

I sat there and listened to my fellow classmates speak. It was all sinking in—I really was done with high school. I had already decided to go on to St. Cloud State University and to major in nursing with a minor in child psychology. I wanted to help kids, just as my nurses had helped me. I thought it would be the right career for me, because I would know how to talk to kids and help them deal with what they were going through. I couldn't wait to start.

The time came for my row to go onto the stage. I could feel my nerves tingling; the butterflies were going crazy in my stomach. I kept my cool and looked out at the crowd, and then I heard "Amy Marie Mareck." As I approached the stage, I talked to myself in my head: *One step at a time, step one, step two, across the stage, shake his hand, down one, down two, walk in front of the crowd, back to your seat.* I had done it! I had made it through without falling on my face.

The ceremony ended, and it was picture time—pictures with family, with friends, and with people I didn't even know. I enjoyed the moment, realizing how hard I had worked to get there.

THAT NIGHT, the school graduation party took place. The gym and commons area were decorated with palm trees, sandals, grass skirts, and everything that went with a beach theme. We played darts, treasure chest, ring toss, and my personal favorite, golf pool (where the golf balls are set up like pool balls and you break from there). The night was filled with fun, friends, laughs, and food. Waiters walked around serving chocolate-covered strawberries and smoothies. We stayed until early morning, and then it was over. It couldn't have gone any better.

Heading home and to bed, I realized that high school was done forever. I was free and on my own. It was up to me to decide what to do with the rest of my life. I was ready to begin the next chapter.

Enjoy school and friends when you can.

School was a challenge but one I welcomed because it was something to focus on other than my medical problems. When I was in school, I felt like a normal person doing normal things. And being in school meant I was with my friends. They were always there for me, in or out of school. They welcomed me with open arms, and we picked right up from wherever we had left off. Treasure your friendships—they're a gift. Enjoy school whenever you can—there is so much to learn.

HAVING CANCER HAS CHANGED my outlook on life. I can honestly say it has changed my life for the better. I don't take anything for granted anymore, and I take time to notice the little things, like a snowflake or the wings of a butterfly. I had never done that before. I live today, remember yesterday, and dream about the future.

If I could paint a picture of my future, it would be like this: go to college and find the guy of my dreams while learning to be the best nurse I could. I'd get a job at a hospital as a nurse's aid or I'd volunteer. I'd finish college, and then move on to nursing school. After graduating from nursing school, I'd begin my career as a nurse at a hospital working on the pediatric floor.

I wanted to set high goals in my life, and I knew that even if it wasn't possible to achieve them all, I'd never stop trying. I was fighting for my life. I would never give up—never. My first goal in life was to beat cancer. It was my dream, my wish, my greatest hope: to beat cancer.

Focus on the good things.

Having cancer stinks—but there are some good things
that come up along the way. You might realize who your
true friends are and grow even closer to your family. You
may make many new friends at the hospital—people you
never would have met otherwise. You will probably meet
an amazing team of doctors, residents, and nurses just like
I did. You may even find ways to participate in fundraising
events for cancer research. Throughout my fight with cancer,
I tried to make the best of a hard situation. I would always
look forward, instead of looking back or dwelling too much
on what I was going through. Cancer is a bad thing, but what
you *do* with it helps determine the outcome. Try to find the
positive in every situation. Cancer can't take your hopes and
dreams away—so live each day to the fullest and dream of
the future. Never give up hope!

Afterword

*"We're changed now. Not because she left us,
but because she touched us."*
—Unknown

Tuesday November 23, 2004, was the day my sister Amy called and told me her scans were terrible. Between Amy and I, we never expected her scans to be clean because there was always something that had changed—a new spot or a spot that had grown. Not yet alarmed, I asked her, "What do you mean, your scans were terrible? Is there another spot? Did one of them grow?"

When she didn't immediately respond to my questions, I knew she was crying on the other end of the phone. The alarms inside me started to go off, and I knew something was wrong—very, very wrong. She finally answered and said, "My right lung is full of cancer." I didn't know what to say. I had to sit down because I suddenly felt overwhelmed with thoughts I had never let myself think before that moment. For five years, I truly believed my sister would win the war against cancer. There was never a doubt in my mind that she would succeed. She had too much drive and determination inside her not to overcome this nightmare she had been living for five years.

I remember finally answering her after collecting my thoughts, saying, "I'm so sorry." She told me there was going to be a meeting the following Tuesday, and she wanted me to come. I told her I would be there, no matter what. We talked for a few minutes after that, and I couldn't even tell you what was said. I was already thinking about what lay ahead of us. This was the first time in five years that I thought my sister wasn't going to make it, and then I was mad at myself for even thinking that thought.

The following day, Amy called me and told me she was having some trouble breathing and wasn't getting enough air; it was making her really nervous. She sounded panicked. She had a fever and showed signs of pneumonia. She wanted to go to the hospital. She said she would feel more comfortable there than at home right now.

Amy was scared, and I was scared for her. But she was always looking forward, never backward, and fighting for her life every step of the way. She was extremely determined to beat this, and I really hoped she could. If anyone could overcome this latest setback, it would be Amy.

On November 25, Thanksgiving Day, Amy called everyone and wished them a Happy Thanksgiving, with a voice barely above a whisper. Something had caused her to lose her voice. Our mom and dad brought her a plate of food from Thanksgiving dinner at Andy and Michele's. She enjoyed it, especially the dressing that tasted similar to our mom's but had "the Michele touch" (that's what Amy said). Amy also enjoyed the mashed potatoes with corn mixed in; she said that was the only way to go. Amy felt better after arriving at the hospital and was more comfortable because she was on oxygen. She continued to spike fevers, which made it hard for her to breathe. Amy spent the day trying to take it easy and not waste any unnecessary energy.

My children, Brittany and Brandon, came with me to visit Amy on the Friday after Thanksgiving. We arrived shortly after lunch, and I remember her wishing that we had gotten there sooner. She was not forgiving of the fact that I had spent the morning shopping (after all, it was the day after Thanksgiving, and I was looking for good deals). The day seemed similar to any other day we had spent with her at the hospital. We spent most of time talking, which was still hard for her because her voice had not returned. The only unusual thing I noticed was that she had made a list of things to talk about. She had never made a list before.

When it was time for us to leave, I remember Amy not wanting us to go. She kept coming up with a reason for us not to leave, things like needing this moved here and that moved there. I can still picture her leaning toward the foot of her bed, looking out the door, and yelling down the hall with hardly any voice, "Denise, Denise, come here!" I would go back one more time to see what it was she still needed. I never minded doing that because it was always hard to leave Amy behind; I always wanted to take her home with me. I told her that Mom and Dad would come bright and early the following morning, so she should try to get some rest.

Amy spent Saturday with our parents, and they all had a great day. Once again she couldn't stop talking; she had so much to say. Her voice hadn't returned yet, so she continued to speak in whispers. That night, Amy was surprised by a group of her closest friends who came to see her; she was so happy and excited about their visit. They hung out for the evening, just as they would have done if they were at home. They ordered pizza and enjoyed each other's company. When it was time for them to go, Amy gave everyone hugs and thanked them for coming; as they left her room, she made them come back for another round of hugs. Amy loved her friends; they always included her and made her feel like a normal teenager, and she knew she could always count on them no matter what.

Our parents stayed overnight at a motel and were back in Amy's room early Sunday morning. By this time, Amy had started to take a turn for the worse. Everything was going way too fast. It was early afternoon when I received a call from our dad saying that if we wanted to spend some quality time with Amy, we should probably come now. I couldn't believe what I was hearing. I had just spent the day with Amy on Friday, and everything had been fine. It had been just another hospital visit, hadn't it? What did he mean by "quality time"? What was happening? Was she dying? I just couldn't grasp it. I thought to myself, *What can I do to slow this down? How do I stop this? I have to help her. No, I must have misunderstood; this just isn't right.*

We packed and headed to the hospital to be with Amy. I couldn't stop crying. I just could not understand how it could be true; I was in total denial—my sister was not dying, now or ever. She was way too strong, too determined, too much of a fighter. No one was going to take her from me. She had slept beside me every night from the moment our parents had brought her home from the hospital when I was a teenager, until the day I moved out four years later. She was my precious sister. I had protected her and loved her, and now I was failing her.

We arrived at the hospital with very heavy hearts. I felt like I was now living inside of Amy's nightmare, and I wanted to wake up. When we arrived, Amy was in good spirits. I think she knew more about what was going on than the rest of us did. She was calm and loving. She was very aware of her surroundings and who was there. I will always remember the moments of laughter and those beautiful dimples that were her pride and joy radiating from her face. I remember when it was just Amy's niece and nephews sitting by her side, and the only thing she said was "Perfect." She loved them so much, and they loved their Auntie Amy right back. The thought of them growing up without her broke my heart. How could God allow this to happen? I thought, *We need her; she's the key to our family, the glue that holds us together.* This had to be an awful dream, and I needed to wake up and make it go away, but it wasn't to be.

Amy had many visitors that day, mostly family and friends. When we left in the evening, I told Amy that I would be back the next day as soon as I could. We said good-bye with lots of hugs, kisses, and "I love you's." Then we left, and I thought to myself, *Tomorrow will be a better day.* I planned on spending the next night with her, and we were going to do the sister-bonding thing. We had a lot to talk about, but we never got that chance.

Everyone had left but Mom, and she and Amy settled in for the night. Amy woke up during the middle of the night, went to the bathroom, crawled back into bed, and told our mom that she loved her. Those were the last words that Amy ever spoke; she drifted off to sleep holding Mom's hand.

The call came at two thirty in the morning, and I was afraid to answer the phone. In fact, I didn't want to answer the phone—I couldn't answer the phone. My husband Dick took the call. It was my dad. The two of them spoke briefly, and then Dick handed the phone to me. I couldn't breathe; my heart was racing, and I couldn't speak.

My dad said that we needed to get to the hospital immediately because Amy's journey was about to head in a new direction that no longer included her family here on earth. I couldn't believe how fast this was going. I had been thinking we would have weeks, months, or more with her. Never, ever did I think that when she had called me on Tuesday, only six days before, that in less than one week I would no longer have my sister.

After a brief conversation with my dad, we once again packed and left for the Twin Cities. By the time we got there, it was five thirty in the morning. Amy was already in a deep sleep. We talked to her and rubbed her hand; we tried anything to make her wake up. We wanted her to wake up one more time so we could tell her how much we loved her.

As we sat with Amy, we noticed a painting hanging on the wall, a picture of an ocean sunrise or sunset that Amy had created. When I looked at it, I could feel the warmth, calm, and peace of that place. I could envision Amy there and, in my mind, it would be her heaven. We later framed the treasured painting, and it hangs on a wall in our parents' home, forever a reminder of Amy.

Finally, after many long hours, Amy woke, but only for a moment. She made eye contact but could not speak. We told her we loved her, we would miss her, and we wanted her to have a safe journey to her new home up in heaven. Twenty minutes later she passed away quietly in her sleep. It was 2:20 in the afternoon on Monday November 29, 2004. Amy was no longer in pain. She no longer had to fight for her life. She was at peace. She was now our beautiful Angel Amy, celebrating her new life up in heaven.

Later that afternoon, my brother and I left a message on Amy's CaringBridge Web site, a site that helped us share news of Amy's fight. We needed to tell everyone the news that was breaking our hearts.

The next few days were barely tolerable as the realization began to sink in: Amy would no longer grace us with her physical presence. My family was brokenhearted beyond words; there was an endless flow of tears shed for our beautiful Amy.

It felt like it couldn't possibly be true that Amy had died. We spent hours sitting in her room listening to the music she had last listened to on her brand new stereo. We sat on her bed, smelled her perfume and lotions, looked at her pictures, and just remembered. It was hard to even function, but we needed to plan the funeral, the celebration of Amy's short yet monumental life. She had lived every day to the fullest with endless energy, strength, and pride. She loved life—she cherished life—and she shared her life with each and every one of us who was touched by her smile, her charm, her warmth, and her love of life.

At first, I found myself angry with God, because how could He take this beautiful girl who had so much to live for? She had so many hopes and dreams. Her life was already mapped out; she was going to go to college and become a nurse at the University of Minnesota Children's Hospital and work on 5B. She wanted to help all the children cope and deal with cancer; she figured her experiences would help them deal with their own. Amy would often say, "I want to help them kick cancer in the butt!" She wanted to volunteer her time and help raise money to fund cancer research. She wanted to get married and have children. She just wanted to live.

I've decided I can't be angry with God because the only way I can deal with this is to believe that Amy was already an angel here on earth and, because she accomplished the goals He set forth for her, it was time for her to go home to God's family, where I'm sure she was welcomed with open arms. I just feel cheated and want her back. She had so much life left to live. She is my sister and I miss her.

Amy's funeral was held on Friday December 3, 2004, at Seven Dolors Church in Albany. If it is any indication how much Amy was loved, hundreds of people came to honor her life. There were beautiful flowers and plants everywhere. Her wake was even held in a gymnasium. I thought, *How appro-priate, one of Amy's favorite sports was basketball, and here we are in a gym honoring Amy among family and friends.* Amy would have been happy. There were many special guests, but one of them came all the way from Philadelphia. Jodi Graubard, whom Amy had gotten to know through her CaringBridge Web site but had never met in person, came to honor Amy. Jodi was the person who had encouraged and motivated Amy to write her book about her life. For this, we all will be forever grateful.

My mom and I shared a special moment the morning of the funeral. As we were walking away from Amy and no one else was around, we happened to look back and noticed a beam of light shining down upon her face. We could only smile because it looked like she was smiling back at us with her beautiful dimples. My mom and I embraced; we both felt it was a sign that she was safe and happy. She had made it to her new home in heaven.

Amy's funeral was a beautiful tribute to her life, with scrip-ture readings and music and a very special eulogy, started by our dad and then given by Amy herself. Back when Amy had participated in the "KS95 for Kids Radiothon" raising money for children's cancer research, she had given an interview telling the story of her life. We played the taped interview with the song "100 Years" by Five for Fighting in the background. It was an Amy moment I will never forget; it made me cry and smile at the same time. She was truly a gift, given to all of us to share for nineteen years, filling our lives with many happy moments. Anyone who took the time to know her understood that she was a treasure worth holding onto. Now we will trea-sure her through our precious memories.

Our hearts may have a hole from the sadness of her passing, but soon they will fill and overflow with her loving memories. She was beautiful both inside and out, and you couldn't help but be drawn to her. She was my hero, as she was to many. She was so brave and had the courage and strength to stand up and fight her disease head-on every step of the way, something not all of us could have done. She never gave up and always believed that someday her miracle would happen. She brought joy and love to everyone she met. She believed there was something to gain from each and every day she lived, even if it was only to give someone a smile and say hi.

We're sad that she's gone but glad that she's cancer-free and enjoying her newfound freedom in heaven. We'll try to live our own lives to the fullest here on earth, knowing that someday we will meet Amy again. She will always be our dear, sweet Angel Amy.

—Denise Waldvogel

The publication of this book was made possible by the generous supporters of Children's Cancer Research Fund.

ABOUT CHILDREN'S CANCER RESEARCH FUND
Children's Cancer Research Fund® is dedicated to finding a cure for childhood cancer by providing critical funding to the University of Minnesota for research and training related to the prevention, treatment, and cure of childhood cancer. The organization also educates the public about childhood cancer and supports quality-of-life programs for pediatric cancer patients and their families.

- One out of every 350 children in the United States develops cancer before age twenty. It is the leading cause of death due to illness in children.

- The median age when children get cancer is six.

- Before 1950, the five-year survival rate was ten percent. Today, nearly eighty percent of children diagnosed with cancer are successfully treated.

Children's Cancer Research Fund® supports cutting-edge research initiatives that lead to larger studies, clinical trials, and improved methods of treating childhood cancer. Researchers are actively studying childhood cancers to better understand their biology and possible causes with the ultimate goal of preventing them.

For more information, visit *www.childrenscancer.org.*

ABOUT CARE PARTNERS

Care Partners is a one-of-a-kind program providing non-medical support to the families of pediatric oncology and blood or marrow transplant patients at the University of Minnesota Children's Hospital, Fairview. Care Partners has served over 2,500 families since its establishment in 1983 and currently has nearly 150 dedicated volunteers.

Clinical volunteers provide art and craft activities for patients and their siblings in the outpatient clinics. Unit volunteers commit to weekly four-hour shifts to stay with patients so that parents get some time out of the hospital room. The heart of the Care Partners program is the family volunteer, who is assigned to one family at a time, becoming a "best friend." Family volunteers provide meals, snacks, transportation, breaks for parents, a listening ear, and, always, a deep level of care and concern.

Care Partners Book Cart provides free books to patients. Since its inception in 2005, the Book Cart program has distributed over 3,000 free books to patients and families.

Support for Care Partners is provided by Children's Cancer Research Fund.

ABOUT UNIVERSITY OF MINNESOTA CANCER CENTER

The University of Minnesota Cancer Center is one of the world's leading institutions for childhood cancer research, treatment, and education. Founded in 1991, and designated a Comprehensive Cancer Center by the National Cancer Institute, the University of Minnesota Cancer Center cares for children from diagnosis through treatment and long-term follow-up care.

Since performing the world's first successful bone marrow transplant for lymphoma in 1975, research at the Cancer

Center has significantly contributed to the care of cancer patients. Advances have included innovative umbilical cord blood transplant regimens, the development of new drugs for treating high-risk or relapsed malignancies, the formation of the Childhood Cancer Survivor Study to better understand the long-term effects of cancer therapy, and the creation of the Long-Term Follow-Up Clinic to provide care for survivors of childhood and young adult cancer.

The Children's Cancer Research Fund has been a continuous partner and generous supporter of the Cancer Center for more than twenty-five years and has helped make these achievements a reality.

For more information about the University of Minnesota Cancer Center, please visit *www.cancer.umn.edu.*

ABOUT UNIVERSITY OF MINNESOTA CHILDREN'S HOSPITAL, FAIRVIEW

University of Minnesota Children's Hospital, Fairview is an internationally renowned facility that treats children with common to complex health conditions.

Located on the east and west banks of the Mississippi River in Minneapolis and affiliated with the University of Minnesota Medical School, University of Minnesota Children's Hospital, Fairview provides a broad spectrum of pediatric programs and services, including surgery, imaging, neonatal and pediatric intensive care, cardiac services, oncology, and transplantation.

UMMCH staff, University of Minnesota Physicians, and community physicians work together to balance innovative technology and treatments with personal concern to address the physical, emotional, cultural, and spiritual needs of pediatric patients and their families.

Visit *uofmchildrenshospital.org* to learn more.